Strength Unto the Battle

also by Brian Miller

Devotions for Cops and the People They Serve

2

Strength Unto the Battle

Brian Miller

The stories in this book are all factual. My memory of all the details isn't perfect, so some details are ad-libbed for clarity. Some names have been changed, and some language cleaned up. All Scriptures are from the King James Bible.

Introduction: Strength Unto the Battle

"For thou hast girded me with strength unto the battle:" (Psalm 18:39)

David knew what it meant to put his life on the line. As a shepherd, he fought bravely against vicious animals who attacked the flock. When he volunteered to fight Goliath and King Saul doubted he could win, David replied,

"Thy servant kept his father's sheep, and there came a lion, and a bear, and took a lamb out of the flock:

And I went out after him, and smote him, and delivered it out of his mouth: and when he arose against me, I caught him by his beard, and smote him, and slew him." (1 Samuel 17:34-35)

As a young patriot, David confronted Goliath when no one else would. As a military commander, he led his troops victoriously. Even after King Saul falsely accused him of trying to usurp the throne and put him on "Israel's Most Wanted" list, David proved himself a worthy leader.

Yet military conflicts weren't David's only battles. When Samuel anointed David king of Israel in front of his older brothers, David had to resist pride. When his three eldest brothers went to fight in Israel's army and David had to stay behind and mind the sheep, he had to resist disobedience and discontentment.

After he killed Goliath, ladies in Israel sang his name,

and Saul made him commander of all Israel's forces—
"...Saul set him over the men of war," (1 Samuel 18:5)—David had to resist pride again. When Saul accused David falsely of trying to usurp the throne and demoted him from commander to *"...captain over a thousand;" (1 Samuel 18:13),* David had to resist bitterness.

When Saul and his troops hunted after David, Saul took a rest in a cave, not knowing that David was behind him about an arm's length away. David had to resist peer pressure to take matters into his own hands and kill Saul.

David fought many battles—including personal battles--in his life. He didn't always win. Nobody *always* wins. Yet through David's life we see God's hand of blessing, guidance, provision, and sometimes chastisement. David testified of God, *"For thou hast girded me with strength unto the battle:" (Psalm 18:39)* Whatever the nature of the battle, God provided David the strength he needed.

Run those ten words through your head a few times: *"For thou hast girded me with strength unto the battle:" (Psalm 18:39)* Why do you think these words are in the Bible? So people could know God gave David strength for his battles? That's nice, but if that were the only reason, what good do these words do us?

Truth is, they're not just there for a history lesson. These words are a promise from God that He'll give us strength for our battles, just as He gave David. *Romans*

2:11 says, *"For there is no respect of persons with God."* God is just as powerful as He was back then. He loves people in this generation just as much as people back then. If God was willing and able to give David the strength he needed, God is willing and able to do the same for us.

As a cop, you'll face battles many people, including many Christians, won't. Some will be physical. Others will be moral and ethical, and still others emotional. Yet whatever the battle, God has promised to give you *"strength unto the battle."* You may not kill any nine-foot giants, but if you'll *"Trust in the LORD, and do good;" (Psalm 37:3)* you'll see many exciting spiritual victories.

This book is not just a set of police stories, but a book of Bible truths to help you trust in the Lord and walk pleasing to Him in your career.

If you aren't sure you'll be in heaven when you die, the first essay will explain from Scripture how to trust Jesus as Saviour. If you already know Jesus as Saviour, I pray the other essays in this book will help you to love His Word and appreciate His grace more than ever.

One essay is from my wife Debbie. If you aren't familiar with the term, "Proverbs 31 Woman", her essay explains it and her life exemplifies it. Thanks also to retired Cleveland Police Lieutenant Patrick Evans, who contributed an essay.

The Heart of the Saviour

"For the Son of man is come to seek and to save that which was lost." (Luke 19:10)

When I was about seven years old one summer, I went to a city swimming pool. I saw kids playing and having a ball. I stepped to the edge and jumped in.

Unfortunately, the water was over my head and I didn't know how to swim. I still remember sinking like a rock. I scrabbled desperately, to no avail. Suddenly, a strong arm grabbed me and pulled me to safety. A lifeguard had seen me drowning and saved me.

I'd made a bad decision to jump into deep water; not a sinful decision, but it was a bad decision that could have cost me my life. Once I jumped, I couldn't undo what was about to happen, and I could have drowned.

The young lady who rescued me was, in a manner of speaking, my saviour (small "s"). She rescued me from the results of my own action. What she did for me is an example of what Jesus did and still does for sinners.

We've all made bad decisions. Maybe they weren't always life-threatening, but we've all made them and done things that are wrong before God. Those actions are called sins. *Romans 3:23* says, *"For all have sinned, and come short of the glory of God;"*

You've said, done, and thought things you shouldn't have. Maybe you think your sins are no worse than anyone else's. Maybe so, but that's not the point. The verse doesn't say, "some have sinned worse than others." It says, *"For all have sinned,"* and so all, even you, have *"come short of the glory of God;"* So, your sins have separated you from a holy God.

Romans 6:23 also says, *"For the wages of sin is death;"* This is the fatal problem that your sin has created for you: condemnation to death. God has set a penalty for sin. The penalty is death. Your sin deserves death, and if you die without your sins forgiven, you'll spend eternity the same way.

The place where people go who die in their sin is the lake of fire: *"And death and hell were cast into the lake of fire. This is the second death." (Revelation 20:14)*

God doesn't want that to happen. If He didn't care about us, He could have put us in hell after our first sin. Yet God also can't just fluff off sin. If He did, He wouldn't be holy. So, how does God reconcile His holiness with His love for sinners?

Here's how. God provided a way for us to be forgiven for our sins by punishing God the Son, the Lord Jesus, in our place: *"For he* [God the Father] *hath made him* [God the Son, Jesus] *to be sin for us, who knew no sin;"* *(2 Corinthians 5:21)*

Jesus was and is God the Son. As God the Son, He never committed any sin. Ever. He even challenged His Pharisee enemies, *"Which of you convinceth me of sin?" (John 8:46)* Of course, none of them could. But Jesus allowed Himself to be falsely arrested, falsely tried, falsely convicted, and falsely executed.

Jesus' death was technically a murder, engineered by the religious leaders. Stephen, a deacon in the early church era, confronted them about *"...the Just One* [Jesus]; *of whom ye have been now the betrayers and murderers:" (Acts 7:52)* They were furious to hear him say that, but they knew it was true.

Jesus let the whole nightmare of His crucifixion play out. As He hung on the cross, as *Isaiah 53:6* says, *"...the LORD* [God the Father] *hath laid on him* [God the Son, Jesus] *the iniquity of us all."* He took the punishment of a holy God for every sin you would ever commit.

Can you imagine having to write down every single sin you'd ever committed in your life, even from when you were a kid? That'd be impossible! Yet Jesus paid for every single one: *"Who his own self bare our sins* [yes, all of them] *in his own body on the tree," (1 Peter 2:24)* Just before Jesus died, He said, *"It is finished:" (John 19:30)* That means the penalty for your sins has been paid in full.

Hebrews 12:2 says Jesus, *"...who for the joy that was*

set before him endured the cross, despising the shame," The Lord didn't mind the shame of the crucifixion. He looked forward to the joy of seeing lost sinners come to Him to be saved.

The lifeguard didn't stand on the edge of the pool complaining, "Look at that stupid kid drowning! Now I have to jump in and get my hair wet!" She jumped in and grabbed me right away! I knew that because it seemed only a few seconds from the time I jumped in to the time she pulled me out. Saving lives wasn't just her job, but in her heart!

In a much greater way, being the Saviour of sinners isn't just Jesus' job. It's in His heart! The lifeguard saved me from the consequences of my decision. In a far greater way, Jesus saves people from the eternal consequences of their sinful decisions!

Luke 19:10 says, *"For the Son of man is come to seek and to save that which was lost."* Jesus didn't just come to save lost people, but to *seek* and to save lost people. If you're bugged about where you'll spend eternity, that's no accident. The Lord is working on your heart. The answer to your uncertainty is to receive the Lord Jesus as YOUR personal Saviour.

He fully paid your sin-debt in full, but in order for the payment to be applied to you, you need to receive Him personally: *"But as many as received him, to them gave he power to become the sons of God, even to them that*

16

believe on his name:" (John 1:12)

To receive the Lord as your personal Saviour means to admit your lost, sinful condition, and come to Him in repentance, which is a turning, a change of mind about your sin where you honestly want forgiveness. You invite Him into your life, trusting Him entirely and from your heart to forgive and save you. If you'll do that, God's Word tells us that four things are guaranteed to happen:

1. **Complete forgiveness of all sins, past present, and future:** *"In whom* [Jesus] *we have redemption through his blood, even the forgiveness of sins:" (Colossians 1:14)*
2. **An eternal home in heaven to look forward to:** *"For the hope which is laid up for you in heaven, whereof ye heard before in the word of the truth of the gospel;" (Colossians 1:5)*
3. **A new birth as a child of God:** *"But as many as received him, to them gave he power to become the sons of God, even to them that believe on his name: Which were born, not of blood, nor of the will of the flesh, nor of the will of man, but of God." (John 1:12-13)*
4. **Jesus' indwelling presence:** *"I am crucified with Christ: nevertheless I live; yet not I, but Christ liveth in me:" (Galatians 2:20)*

You can make that decision right where you are. If you've decided to receive the Lord Jesus, you could call on Him like this: *"Lord Jesus, I know I'm a sinner and deserve hell. But your death paid for all my sins, and you were buried and rose again. Forgive me my sins. I repent. I'm inviting you into my heart and life right now to be my personal Saviour. I'm trusting entirely in you to get me to heaven when I die. Thank you, Lord Jesus."*

If you've received Jesus as Saviour, you can now look at those verses previously listed and say confidently that they apply to you: that your sins are all forgiven, Jesus is now your personal Saviour, and heaven is your eternal home.

Growing in Grace

"But grow in grace, and in the knowledge of our Lord and Saviour Jesus Christ." (2 Peter 3:18)

The apostle Peter wrote two letters, or epistles, to believers in Jesus, *1 Peter* and *2 Peter,* respectively. At the end of *2 Peter*, he told believers to grow in grace, as our verse says.

For the sake of clarity, God saves people by His grace:

"For by grace are ye saved through faith; and that not of yourselves: it is the gift of God: Not of works, lest any man should boast." (Ephesians 2:8-9)

First you see from the Bible that you're a sinner and deserve hell. Then you see that God the Son, Jesus Christ, died to pay for all your sins, was buried, and rose again. When you receive Jesus as Saviour, He saves you and you now have eternal life. It's a gift of God's grace, not a result of your works, like our above passage tells us.

God saves people by grace, but God also wants us to grow in grace, like our verse says: *"But grow in grace,"* To grow in grace means to become more mature as Christians and more like Jesus. *Romans 8:29* says, *"...*[God] *did predestinate* [Christians] *to be conformed to the image of his Son,"*

19

The moment you receive Jesus as Saviour, you're as much saved and a Christian as anyone else who's received Jesus as Saviour. As soon as you came to Jesus in repentance and faith, He saved you right then:

"And the transaction so quickly was made,
when as a sinner I came,
took of the offer of grace he did proffer,
He saved me, O praise His dear name."
"Heaven Came Down" by John W. Peterson

Yet you may not know what you should do as a Christian; It's like, "Ok, I'm saved. Now what?" You're saved by grace and have eternal life, but you also need to grow in grace.

To illustrate the point, let's take young Officer Smith. He's passed the academy and his probation period, so he's officially the police. Unfortunately, Smith has a bit of a "store-bought" attitude. He wants to be like senior cops, so he tries to act "salty." Maybe you know some young officers like that. Maybe you were like that yourself.

Here's a "store bought" attitude, by the way: When I had about four and a-half years on, I saw an academy classmate at another district. He said he was on "the retirement shift." That's a "store bought" attitude. He didn't get that attitude by experience. He only had four and a-half years on. He picked it up from others.

Back to Officer Smith: Smith is as much a police officer as an experienced veteran, but he needs to mature. As he spends more time on the job and grows in knowledge and job skills—as well as people skills—he'll be more mature as an officer.

That's how it is with Christian growth. There are no perfect Christians, just as there are no perfect police officers. Christian growth is not a goal we reach, where one day we're perfect. Rather, it's a continual process, or should be, in our lives. We won't be perfectly Christ-like in this life, but when we see Jesus, we will be: *"...we shall be like him; for we shall see him as he is."* *(1 John 3:2)*

Who's Smarter, You or God?

"...if they speak not according to this word, it is because there is no light in them." (Isaiah 8:20)

One night a police chaplain was with me on a ride-along. The ride seemed amiable enough, but when it came time to drop him off, he told me clear out of the blue—and he wasn't smiling as he said it--"I don't talk to people out of a book."

It was obvious to me that the book he was talking about was the Bible. It was no secret on the department that I was a Bible thumper. Info like that tends to go viral because cops can be gossips.

I'm not sure how I replied, if I replied at all. In a way, his comment didn't bother me. I didn't belong to his religion. I also had several years on the job and my faith in the Lord and in His Word was still intact.

I also understood—in a general sense--about not talking out of a book. If you want to talk with cops and have credibility, book knowledge isn't enough. You need experience under your belt. You need to be able to say, "I've been where you've been."

It's also true that cops don't always go by the book. In the inner city, especially, you have to choose your battles. For example, if you see cars parked on Sunday morning on the treelawn outside a small church with very little parking space, don't write parking tickets.

When it comes to the Bible, though, you have to go by the book. God gave us the Bible so we could know what He's about. If God hadn't done that, we'd be at the mercy of every religious con artist that came down the pike. There would be confusion, and *"...God is not the author of confusion," (1 Corinthians 14:33)*

So, if a minister thinks the Bible is just a book, as the chaplain obviously did, and doesn't respect it as God's Word, what does he use to counsel people or preach sermons? His imagination? Is he smarter than God?

People in Old Testament Israel had the same problem. They would disregard God's law and adopt the religious customs of the heathen people around them. Disregarding God's Word was a bad idea then. It still is now.

God gave us His Word. We can trust Him to be true to His Word. God also ordained law and order: *"...the powers that be are ordained of God." (Romans 13:1)* That also means He ordained police work, so if you're a cop, you're working a job that God Himself ordained.

Don't ever believe you can't live for Christ as a cop. If it's God's will for you to be a cop, it's God's will for you to live for Christ as a cop. Living for Christ as a cop can be tough but it can be tough anywhere. That's why it's called *"...the good **fight** of faith," (1 Timothy*

6:12, boldface added)

You'll face things as a cop most people won't ever face, but you'll never face anything the Lord can't or won't give you grace to deal with. Jesus said, *"My grace is sufficient for thee:" (2 Corinthians 12:9)* Paul also said in *Philippians 4:13, "I can do **all things** [boldface added] through Christ which strengtheneth me."* These are God's Words. He doesn't lie.

If you want to be a strong Christian in any walk of life, what you do with God's Word is crucial. It's God's source of grace for you. Spend time in it. Read it. Memorize it. Think about its truths often. Believe it. Obey it. *1 John 2:14* says, *"...I have written unto you, young men, because ye are strong, and the word of God abideth in you, and ye have overcome the wicked one."*

The Case for the Risen Christ

"For I delivered unto you first of all that which I also received, how that Christ died for our sins according to the scriptures; And that he was buried, and that he rose again the third day according to the scriptures:" *(1 Corinthians 15:3-4)*

The burden of proof for criminal prosecution is "beyond a reasonable doubt." When you make a case, you want your case to be as airtight as possible. You don't want to leave any opening for a defense attorney to create reasonable doubt in the minds of the jurors.

That said, let's look at the central truth of the Christian faith: the resurrection of Jesus. If Jesus didn't rise, the Christian faith is vain: *"And if Christ be not risen, then is our preaching vain, and your faith is also vain."* *(1 Corinthians 15:14)* God gave us plenty of evidence in His Word to prove the case for the resurrection of Jesus.

First, it proves that Jesus is the Son of God, God in the flesh. Here are just a few things Jesus did that only God can do:

a. He accepted worship, which only God deserves: *"And he* [a man blind from birth to whom Jesus gave sight] *said* [to Jesus], *Lord, I believe. And he worshipped him."* *(John 9:38)*

b. He also had power to forgive sins, which only God can do: *"When Jesus saw their faith, he said unto the sick of the palsy, Son, thy sins be forgiven thee."* (Mark 2:5)

c. He also said, *"...I lay down my life, that I might take it again. No man taketh it from me, but I lay it down of myself."* (John 10:17-18) A man can't lay down his own life and take it again, but God can.

Jesus' resurrection also proves His death atoned for sins. The cup at the Last Supper symbolized His blood: *"For this is my blood of the new testament, which is shed for many for the remission* [forgiveness] *of sins."* (Matthew 26:28)

Jesus also didn't just say He'd die for sins, but He'd die for sins *and rise again.* If He hadn't risen, His death would have meant nothing. But He did rise, which proves He was telling the truth and His death did pay for sins.

His enemies remembered He'd promised to rise again, so after He was crucified, they asked Pilate to post a guard at the tomb: not to keep Him in, but to keep His disciples from taking His body and spreading a rumor that He'd risen from the dead. They didn't think He'd rise again, but He did! He proved by His resurrection that He was who He said He was and that His death accomplished what He'd said it would.

After Jesus rose, He appeared to over 500 believers. He let them touch Him: *"Behold my hands and my feet, that it is I myself: handle me, and see; for a spirit hath not flesh and bones, as ye see me have."* (Luke 24:39) He showed them His through-and-through nail scars. He even ate! *"And they gave him a piece of a broiled fish, and of an honeycomb. And he took it, and did eat before them."* (Luke 24:42-43)

When Jesus came out of the tomb, the guards couldn't do a thing about it. They were terrified: *"And for fear of him the keepers did shake, and became as dead men."* (Matthew 28:4)

Look what happened next!

"Now when they were going, behold, some of the watch came into the city, and shewed unto the chief priests all the things that were done. And when they were assembled with the elders, and had taken counsel, they gave large money unto the soldiers, Saying, Say ye, His disciples came by night, and stole him away while we slept. And if this come to the governor's ears, we will persuade him, and secure you. So they took the money, and did as they were taught: and this saying is commonly reported among the Jews until this day." (Matthew 28:11-15)

Can you see the color draining from the chief priests' faces when the guards told them, "The tomb we were guarding, the man came out of it!" Talk about a "wish

I had a camera" moment! They had to do something, so they made up a story and bribed the guards to go along with it. Of course, that did no good. The word went viral: Jesus is risen!

Jesus' resurrection also proves that He's alive! *"I am he that liveth, and was dead; and, behold, I am alive for evermore, Amen;" (Revelation 1:18)*

If you go to the grave of some great past leader and ask for wisdom or help, you'll get no answer. They were only human and they're dead. But if you call on Jesus in repentance to forgive you your sins and save you, trusting Him to do it, He will! He's the Son of God and the living Saviour! He always keeps His promises! *"For whosoever shall call upon the name of the Lord shall be saved. How then shall they call on him in whom they have not believed?" (Romans 10:13-14)*

The gospel is *"...the power of God unto salvation to every one that believeth;" (Romans 1:16)*

A Sure Hope

"Now our Lord Jesus Christ himself, and God, even our Father, which hath loved us, and hath given us everlasting consolation and good hope through grace, Comfort your hearts, and stablish you in every good word and work." (2 Thessalonians 2:16-17)

Police work isn't just a job. It's a vocation for people who are passionate about fighting criminals and helping decent people.

Nowadays, though, it's tougher to do. Cops are more restricted. They don't want to overstep some departmental rule and be suspended and lose money trying to do a good job or be in a high-profile incident and have their life picked apart on TV by media vultures.

All of that is good news for criminals, who have more freedom to prey on decent people who desperately need police service and can't get it. Police departments nationwide are also struggling to recruit new officers, and fewer cops are available to handle calls. Cops are also assaulted and killed on a regular basis.

Will things get better? We can hope, but it may not happen. If you have any amount of time on the job, you may just hope to make it to retirement.

God's Word has a much better hope. Our passage

says God has given us *"everlasting consolation and good hope through grace."* God's consolation is not just temporary, but *everlasting.* His hope is also a *good* hope. We have no sure hope for things to get better as far as the crime rate, but there is a sure hope for eternity.

God's hope is not a cross-your-fingers "maybe" hope. A "maybe" hope is also a "maybe not" hope. That's not a good hope. God's hope is a good hope because it's a sure hope. We have a guarantee of a good hope through the Lord Jesus Christ.

God's hope for eternity is a sure hope because it's based on God's Word and on what Jesus did for us on the cross. All of us have sinned against God. *"For all have sinned, and come short of the glory of God;"* *(Romans 3:23)* So because we've sinned and come short of the glory of God, we can't get into heaven on our own because heaven is God's home and it's holy and we're sinful.

In fact, our sins have also brought condemnation of death and hell on us: *"For the wages of sin is death;"* *"And death and hell were cast into the lake of fire."* *(Romans 6:23, Revelation 20:14)*

But God didn't leave us without hope. He provided a way for us to be forgiven for our sins and be in heaven with Him. *"For God so loved the world, that he gave his only begotten Son, that whosoever believeth in him should not perish, but have everlasting life." (John 3:16)*

God the Son, Jesus Christ, went to the cross and took God's death penalty for our sins: *"Who his own self bare our sins in his own body on the tree," (1 Peter 2:24)* Jesus was buried, rose again the third day, and is now alive! *"I am he that liveth, and was dead; and, behold, I am alive for evermore, Amen;" (Revelation 1:18)*

When a sinner comes to Jesus in repentance and faith and trusts in Him as personal Saviour, Jesus gives pardon for sins and eternal life: *"Verily, verily, I say unto you, He that believeth on me hath everlasting life." (John 6:47)*

Jesus promised. He never lied and never will, and He doesn't play games with people's souls. You may not be hopeful about how things are on the job, but with Jesus as Saviour, you have God's good hope for eternity.

The Devil's Disciples

"And there came a messenger unto Job, and said, The oxen were plowing, and the asses feeding beside them: And the Sabeans fell upon them, and took them away; yea, they have slain the servants with the edge of the sword; and I only am escaped alone to tell thee."
(Job 1:14-15)

Job was a faithful servant of God. One day Satan challenged God. He said Job only served God because God protected him, but if God let Job's goods be harmed, Job would curse God to his face.

Satan asked God's permission to mess with Job. God gave it, and the devil went to work. Our opening passage describes the first thing that happened. A group known as the Sabeans attacked Job's property. The servants were farming and caring for the livestock. The Sabeans stole Job's livestock and murdered his servants in cold blood.

The Bible doesn't tell us much about the Sabeans. Just from this passage, we see that some of them were part of a violent criminal gang.

Imagine the scene after they left: dead bodies, gushing wounds, blood everywhere. If you've had to handle a gory death scene, you probably still remember it in detail years after the fact. We had a call in 1983 of a kid who'd put a shotgun in his mouth and pulled the trigger. I still remember that kid's body today.

In November 1959, two ex-convicts invaded a home in Kansas. They held the family members hostage: a couple and two teenage kids. Ultimately, they brutally murdered all four. Truman Capote wrote his book *In Cold Blood* about this incident.

Back to our Scripture: Satan uses people willing to do wrong. The incident at Job's place was unbelievably brutal, like the incident in Kansas. The massacre at Job's place may not have been the first time the Sabeans had done something like this.

So why did they pick Job's property this time? Because Satan enticed them to do it. They may never have thought of it that way. They probably just heard that some rich guy named Job had property and money, so they did what they did. They may not have known or cared if there were a God or a devil, but they were Satan's flunkies: serving him, doing his dirty work.

So, what can you do with this passage? You could share it with someone you arrest, especially if you've arrested him for a violent crime and especially if he's in a gang. Ask him at the booking window, "How does it feel to serve Satan?"

Ask in a serious way, not joking. He may look at you funny or mumble some profanities. If he does, tell him, "no, really, I'm sincere" and share the story of the

Sabeans. He may be shocked that a cop knows anything about the Bible, but maybe—just maybe—he'll listen.

Hebrews 4:12 says, *"For the word of God is quick, and powerful, and sharper than any two-edged sword, piercing even to the dividing asunder of soul and spirit, and of the joints and marrow, and is a discerner of the thoughts and intents of the heart."*

God's Word deals powerfully with people's hearts. Never underestimate the power of the Word of God.

So why would you care enough about him to say that? Because you're the police. You're the good guy, remember? You risk your life fighting criminals, and unlike criminals, you care about people. You don't want people destroyed if you can help avoid it.

Your suspect may go on in his criminal career and end up being shot to death by a homeowner, the police, or even another criminal. People might tie flowers and teddy bears to a pole for him, but if he died without Christ, he'll be screaming and burning in hell with the devil that he'd served. You don't want that, do you? Of course not.

By sharing the story of the Sabeans, you're really showing him love, "tough love", certainly more love than his buddies do. Wouldn't it be great to learn later that he went straight and even accepted Christ because a cop shared Scripture with him?

'Fessing Up

"...let us cleanse ourselves from all filthiness of the flesh and spirit, perfecting holiness in the fear of God." (2 Corinthians 7:1)

Being saved doesn't make you perfect. Saved people still struggle with sin. Even Paul the apostle did. This passage came from his second letter to the Christians at the church at Corinth. Notice he didn't say, "You people need to cleanse yourselves", but *"...let US cleanse OURSELVES..."* (capitals mine).

We can be tempted in words, deeds, and even thoughts. Sometimes we give in to them. *Hebrews 12:1* even talks about *"...the sin which doth so EASILY (capitals mine) beset us,"* So how do we "cleanse ourselves?" By confessing sin to God when it happens: not to a man, but to God: *"...I will confess my transgressions unto the LORD;" (Psalm 32:5)*

Our verse talks about *"...filthiness of the flesh and spirit"*. Some sins are outward in *"the flesh"*, like alcohol, tobacco, fornication, profanity, gambling, and pornography. Others are in the heart, *"the spirit"*, like hatred, jealousy, unkindness, and bitterness. Both are offensive to God.

The "inside" sins may not show, but fester in the heart like a cancer. God still knows about them: *"...he knoweth the secrets of the heart." (Psalm 44:21)* Both kinds need to be confessed when we see them in our lives.

God promises to forgive us our sins and to cleanse us if we'll confess them honestly: *"If we confess our sins, he is faithful and just to forgive us our sins, and to cleanse us from all unrighteousness." (1 John 1:9)*

Maybe you struggle with some sin that would shock people if they knew about it. Well, God already knows, and He's not shocked. If you're saved, He'll forgive and cleanse you of it. But you need to confess it.

You may find yourself repeating a sin and confessing it again and again. Well, God will never say, "WHAT? THAT SIN AGAIN? I WON'T FORGIVE YOU THIS TIME!" If God did that, He'd be breaking His promise and making Himself a liar. God *"...cannot lie," (Titus 1:2)* So make a habit of confessing known sin to God and trust Him to forgive and cleanse you, as He promised.

Profane language is a good example of a sinful habit that's tough to kick. Some believers in Colosse obviously had this problem. That's why Paul said, *"But now ye also put off all these; anger, wrath, malice, blasphemy, filthy communication out of your mouth." (Colossians 3:8)*

It's very easy for a cop to have a dirty mouth. You deal with dirty-mouthed people all the time. You can also be tempted in the heat of a dangerous or stressful situation to let a dirty word or two slip out.

So, how do you put off filthy talk from your life? Like the Nike commercial says, "Just do it". Profanity offends the Lord and is a lousy testimony. Decide that it won't be a part of your vocabulary anymore. If you slip here or there, stop and ask the Lord to forgive you. If you tend to use bad language in the heat of emotion, ask Him to help you resist the temptation.

God is a merciful God: *"For thou, Lord, art good, and ready to forgive; and plenteous in mercy unto all them that call upon thee."* *(Psalm 86:5)* God wants to forgive sins. Yet God wants honesty. Don't try to cover up sin or excuse it: *"He that covereth his sins shall not prosper:"* *(Proverbs 28:13)* Confess sin when you've done it.

The Better Business Bureau provides quality reports on businesses. The BBB tells consumers not only to note the number of complaints a company has but how they handled them. A company may have a few complaints but still have a good reputation if they handled the complaints to the customer's satisfaction.

In a way, that's like sin in a believer's life. No one is sin-free, just like it'd be tough for a company to be complaint-free. What matters more is what you do with the sin. When you see that you're guilty of it, then handle it to God's satisfaction. Confess it to Him.

Growing through Experience

"But grow in grace, and in the knowledge of our Lord and Saviour Jesus Christ." (2 Peter 3:18)

Our way to grow in grace is to take Scripture truths and apply them to your daily behavior. Paul the apostle said, *"That I may know him* [Jesus]*," (Philippians 3:10)* Paul knew Jesus as Saviour, but he wanted to know Him better. We'll never know the Lord completely until we get to heaven, but we can get to know Him better day by day, by taking Bible truths and applying them to our life.

The Bible revolutionizes people's thinking. When you first heard about being sure of heaven, did you believe it was possible to know for sure? If not, it was likely because you didn't know the Bible very well.

Yet if you took time to hear the gospel and you received Jesus as Saviour, you now can be certain according to the Bible that you'll be in heaven. Verses like Jesus' own words in *John 6:47- "Verily, verily, I say unto you, He that believeth on me hath everlasting life."* give you that assurance.

Yet that's only the beginning of the Christian life. When you read the Bible, God speaks to your heart: to encourage, instruct, challenge, comfort, teach, convict, and whatever else is necessary for you.

Just as you applied Bible principles about salvation to your life by receiving Jesus as Saviour, you need to take Bible principles for your daily life the same way.

Romans 12:2 tells us to be *"...transformed by the renewing of your mind, that ye may prove what is that good, and acceptable, and perfect, will of God."* Having your mind renewed is not a one-time event, but a continual process. It means that now you're a Christian, you need to learn to think like one. You do that by obeying what the Bible says about your conduct; basically, by saying, "this is what the Bible says I should do, so I'll do it."

Colossians 3:10 tells us to be *"...renewed in knowledge* [knowledge of God's Word, the Bible] *after the image of him that created him:" (Colossians 3:10)* The Bible doesn't just give us knowledge, but knowledge to change our minds, behaviors, and lives.

You may read about things that should be in your life, like faithful church attendance, Bible reading, prayer, witnessing and service. Or things that shouldn't be in your life, like wrong talk, bad habits, or ungodly entertainment. As you obey God's Word, you grow as a Christian because you learn to think like one.

As a cop, you learn to think like a cop, to discern behaviors that tell you someone has something to hide. Some are better at it than others. I wasn't good at it, at least not at first.

With a little over a year on the job, I had a traffic stop. A guy in the car had no I.D. but he gave me his Social Security number, except for the last two digits which he said he couldn't remember. I told the dispatcher the guy couldn't remember the last two digits. A cop on another car said over the air, "book him."

He probably had a warrant, but I didn't have the street-smarts to know that a) most people should know their SSN and b) if someone can remember the first seven, he should be able to remember the last two.

Yet knowledge comes with experience. Over time I learned, among other things, to watch people's movements for subtle danger indicators. I can't say how many times I'd catch a slight body movement and end up recovering a gun or contraband. "Watch the hands" is an old piece of advice for cops but still vital for survival and effective police work.

Just as you learn police work—and enjoy it more— by learning and doing, you enjoy your Christian life more—and know your Saviour better--by learning what God's Word says and doing it.

"More about Jesus in His Word, holding communion with my Lord,
Hearing His voice in every line, making each faithful saying mine."
"More about Jesus", Eliza E. Hewitt, John R. Sweney

Helping Us Help Others

"Blessed be God, even the Father of our Lord Jesus Christ, the Father of mercies, and the God of all comfort; Who comforteth us in all our tribulation, that we may be able to comfort them which are in any trouble, by the comfort wherewith we ourselves are comforted of God." (2 Corinthians 1:3-4)

The Bible never says saved people are spared from the problems of life. Jesus said in *Matthew 5:45, "...he* [God] *maketh his sun to rise on the evil and on the good, and sendeth rain on the just and on the unjust."* So saved people are not immune from life's problems.

In fact, saved people who strive to live for Christ may have more problems: *"Yea, and all that will live godly in Christ Jesus shall suffer persecution." (2 Timothy 3:12)* Of course, the easy way to avoid persecution is not to live for Christ, but that wouldn't please the Lord.

Back to how God *"...maketh his sun to rise on the evil and on the good, and sendeth rain on the just and on the unjust."* Saved cops are just as likely as unsaved cops to go through the ordeals that cops go through.

The difference is that saved cops have a source of comfort and help that unsaved cops don't: Jesus Himself. God *"...comforteth us* [believers] *in all our tribulation,"* He doesn't keep us from problems, but He's with us through them: *"God is our refuge and* strength, a very present help in trouble." (Psalm 46:1) Not an absent help, but a PRESENT help in trouble.

When you know Jesus as Saviour, His Word reminds you of His presence and willingness to help you in tough times: *"Fear thou not; for I am with thee: be not dismayed; for I am thy God: I will strengthen thee; yea, I will help thee; yea, I will uphold thee with the right hand of my righteousness." (Isaiah 41:10)*

God also promises that when the trial is over, you will be better for His service than before. Job served God faithfully, but his property was invaded, livestock stolen, servants massacred, his seven sons died in a house collapse, and he was covered with boils head to foot. Yet he said, *"But he* [God] *knoweth the way that I take: when he hath tried me, I shall come forth as gold." (Job 23:10)*

If you've been through dangerous or difficult situations on the job, you're better equipped to help other cops who go through the same thing later. So, God *"...comforteth us in all our tribulation, that we may be able to comfort them which are in any trouble, by the comfort wherewith we ourselves are comforted of God." (2 Corinthians 1:4)*

So when you know Jesus as Saviour and you're going through some trial, the Lord is with you to help you and "refine" you like gold, so you can turn around and help someone else going through a trial.

Willful Ignorance

"And he [Jesus] *called the multitude, and said unto them, Hear, and understand: Not that which goeth into the mouth defileth a man; but that which cometh out of the mouth, this defileth a man. Then came his disciples, and said unto him, Knowest thou that the Pharisees were offended, after they heard this saying? But he answered and said, Every plant, which my heavenly Father hath not planted, shall be rooted up. Let them alone: they be blind leaders of the blind. And if the blind lead the blind, both shall fall into the ditch."* *(Matthew 15:10-14)*

The Pharisees saw Jesus' disciples eating without washing their hands first. They were offended, not for the sake of sanitation but because the disciples were violating a man-made religious tradition.

When they told Jesus of His disciples' violation, He wasn't impressed. He pointed out how they'd disobeyed God by making man-made tradition more important than God's Word. He also told them that their worship of God was just an outward show: *"This people draweth nigh unto me with their mouth, and honoureth me with their lips; but their heart is far from me."* *(Matthew 15:8)*

Jesus didn't care that they were offended. They were misleading people with false doctrine. Jesus called them on it. He did the right thing, the right way. Jesus

43

showed kindness and compassion many times, but this wasn't the time for kindness and compassion. It was a time to call sin by its name.

The Pharisees didn't want to listen to the Lord. Jesus' reply? *"Let them alone: they be blind leaders of the blind."* Their worst problem wasn't ignorance of the truth. It was WILLFUL ignorance and refusal to accept the truth. So, the Lord let them go their way.

You've probably heard people criticize cops, maybe in personal conversation or by some talking head on TV. Not uncommonly, they've never worked as cops and never will, but they have their opinions. The First Amendment gives the right to free speech. It doesn't require that people know what they're talking about.

Maybe you'd tried to argue with some critic, but realized it was a waste of time. When people are willing to admit the truth, though, it's refreshing.

Two protest activists agreed to participate in police deadly force training where *they* played the cop. Both saw deadly force from the cop's point of view. Both had the integrity to agree how scary these situations are (Fox 10 Phoenix, "Activist Critical of Police Undergoes Use of Force Scenarios", by Troy Hayden; and "Minister Quanell X Reactions after going through a police 'shoot don't shoot' exercise", the Steve Malzberg Show).

Some people are the same way about the Bible. Just as those who've never been cops may criticize cops, some who have never read the Bible may criticize the Bible. They may read books *about* the Bible, or criticisms against the Bible, but they've never taken time to read the Bible itself.

God's challenge to people like that is to *"Seek ye out of the book of the LORD, and read:" (Isaiah 34:16)* One reason God inspired His Word is to help people have strong faith in Him by reading it and trusting it.

You may not believe God created everything, or that He gave His only begotten Son Jesus to die for sins and be the Saviour of the world. You lack faith. The remedy for lack of faith is to read the Bible. Don't just read books about the Bible. READ FROM THE BIBLE. That's why *Romans 10:17* says, *"So then faith cometh by hearing, and hearing by the word of God."*

How does faith come? By *"hearing."* Hearing what? *"...the word of God."* You may be a Christian but feel your faith is weak. The answer for you is the same. Spend time in God's Word to strengthen your faith.

On-the-Go Prayer

"Pray without ceasing." (1 Thessalonians 5:17)

When you think of prayer, what do you think of? Maybe, "Now I lay me down to sleep, I pray the Lord my soul to keep; if I should die before I wake, I pray the Lord my soul to take." Or maybe "God is great, God is good, now we thank Him for our food. Amen."

The problem of reciting prayer is that it can become a mindless exercise, what Jesus called, "vain repetitions ": *"But when ye pray, use not vain repetitions," (Matthew 6:7)* Prayer should be from the heart. That's why *Psalm 62:8* says, *"...pour out your heart before him* [God]:"

When you pray, you're asking God to put His Almighty hand into some important issue. You should talk to Him reverently, but also from the heart.

Say you're on patrol. Suddenly the radio bursts into life: *"Any car able to respond, East 55 and Woodland, the gas station was just robbed. Suspect has a white t-shirt, blue jeans, silver handgun, dark Chevy going east on Woodland."* Your adrenaline starts to flow. You grab the mic: *"Radio, we're rolling."*

You hit the overhead lights and put the gas pedal to the floor. Other units are responding. Your heart is racing but you focus on your job as you dodge, weave, and speed to the crime scene. You listen to the radio for more info.

One more thing you can do: pray. Pray to get there safely. Pray for the police to get the victory. Pray for the suspects to get caught. Pray for no one to get hurt.

You don't have to close your eyes or stop. God knows you need to focus on your job. God sees your heart: *"...the LORD looketh on the heart." (1 Samuel 16:7)*

If you're a detective working a case, you may have followed all your leads, held interviews, and combed your cases as best you can. But pray. Pray for witnesses to come forward. Pray for the suspect to make some mistake and get caught. Pray for breaks. Pray for God to do something only He can do.

As a cop, you deal with some of the most wicked people in the world. Maybe you're trying to prosecute some serial child rapist. You might pray something like, "Lord, I'd really like to take this guy and beat him to a pulp. Please help me to resist temptation and do what's right, so we can get him off the street."

One night late in December 2006, a man was shot to death in front of the Glenville YMCA. He was well-loved in the community, and people wanted the killer caught. I was a patrol boss at the time on night shift.

About a week later, Mike Legg received a tip that the

suspect was at a party on Tacoma Avenue. I detailed several cars to meet me at Lakeview and Durant, which was about half a mile away. I had about six officers with me, ready to hit the house on my say-so, but I didn't have peace about it. I needed to stop and pray.

Well, the Lord dealt with my heart. Sure, I wanted to snatch up the suspect, and the guys were willing to go on my order. But if we had tried it and armed gang members had been inside that house, we could have had multiple police shootings at one time.

I couldn't do something stupid and let these young guys get killed. I had to swallow my pride. I called the Special Services Commander, Gary Gingell, and asked for SWAT. He sent a team to help us. So, we waited.

Meanwhile, Vice Sergeant Jim Purcell came with two of his guys, Tim Clark and Ali Pillow. As we waited for SWAT, a citizen pulled up in his pickup. He was frantic. The suspect had left the party and was walking north on East 105 near Gooding Avenue, not far away: dark blue jumpsuit, red rag on his head. We scrambled into our cars and swarmed the area.

As I headed south on East 105 toward Gooding, I saw a small black male with a blue jump suit and red rag on his head, walking on the west side of the street. As he approached Gooding, I turned right suddenly and stopped in his way. I drew my 9mm and pointed it at him. "PUT 'EM UP!" I ordered.

He spun and ran across the street. I jumped out of my car and chased him on foot. As he crossed East 105, I saw him reaching into a leg pocket.

Uh oh. Looks like he's reaching for something.

He rounded the corner of Gooding Avenue on the other side. Car 612 pulled up. Mike Zubal stopped the car. Andy Crytzer bailed out and joined in the chase. Tim and Ali pulled up and joined Andy.

The suspect rounded a building and ran north. He could have pulled a gun in that moment when they lost sight of him, but they pursued. Around the corner, he reached a brick wall and had nowhere else to go. He surrendered.

Once he'd left the party, we no longer had the risk of multiple suspects. We also had so many cops in the area that the suspect was hopelessly outnumbered and outgunned. Yet beyond what the officers did, and they were all great, I'm so grateful that the Lord answers prayer. *Ephesians 3:20* says, *"Now unto him that is able to do exceeding abundantly above all that we ask or think, according to the power that worketh in us,"*

God's willingness to answer prayer isn't limited to our willingness to ask. *Romans 8:26* says, *"...for we know not what we should pray for as we ought:"* So even if we mean well, we may not be praying for the right thing or in the right way. But God can answer our prayer exceedingly abundantly ABOVE our ability to pray or even think.

You may have great police instincts, but God has better police instincts. So, pray for His help on the job. You'll be amazed and your faith will be strengthened when you see how He answers prayer: *"...my heart trusted in him, and I am helped: therefore my heart greatly rejoiceth; and with my song will I praise him."* *(Psalm 28:7)*

Growing with Good Nutrition

"Wherefore laying aside all malice, and all guile, and hypocrisies, and envies, and all evil speakings, As newborn babes, desire the sincere milk of the word, that ye may grow thereby:" (1 Peter 2:1-2)

The apostle Peter told believers in Christ to *"...grow in grace," (2 Peter 3:18)* He also told us how to do that. He was apparently speaking to some new Christians, because he said, *"As newborn babes, desire the sincere milk of the word, that ye may grow thereby:"*

To grow as a Christian, to grow in grace, you need to feed consistently on *"the sincere milk of the word";* that is, the Word of God.

When someone first accepts Jesus as his Saviour, he may not know much about the Bible. Even if he is older when he accepts Christ, he is still, like Peter said, a spiritual "newborn babe" who needs to be fed from God's Word to grow and become strong.

A newborn baby starts out with milk. In the same way, new believers—and older ones--need "spiritual milk." That's basic Bible instruction about Jesus' life, faith in God's Word, prayer, and service. Most of the New Testament, as well as Psalms and Proverbs, are easy to understand and have good basic food that believers need.

By way of example, rookies often don't know much about police work, but they're excited about it, which is great. That's why lazy cops should not train rookies. Young cops don't need lazy veterans filling their heads with whining about how messed-up the job is.

A rookie needs to hear how to do the job right, so he'll grow as an officer. In the same way, a young Christian needs to spend time in God's Word and hear it preached in church, so he'll grow as a Christian.

Here's another police-related example: it's easy to get into the bad habit of eating fast food on the job, especially on night shift, instead of nutritious food from home. Fast food is easy to grab, and you probably get a discount at the fast food place. Yet too much fast food is bad for you. So, take a little time to prepare food from home, and save some money in the process.

Peter also said to *"desire the sincere milk of the word",* which means that it's possible *not* to desire the word. Interestingly, Christians can love the Bible but struggle with making time to read it. Bible reading can be lost in the shuffle of life, especially for cops.

Yet the Bible can become something you actually enjoy. The way for that to happen is for you to read from it, memorize Scriptures that you particularly enjoy, and think often about what you've memorized. Even when you can't read a Bible, you can recall Scriptures that you've memorized, and they'll help you. That way, Scripture is a gift that keeps on giving.

You may not always enjoy reading and memorizing Scripture, but the more you do it, the more you enjoy it and develop a taste for it. *Proverbs 2:10-11* says, *"When wisdom entereth into thine heart, and knowledge is pleasant unto thy soul; Discretion shall preserve thee, understanding shall keep thee:"*

So, it's possible for knowledge from the Bible NOT to be pleasant to your soul. Yet the more you read and memorize it and the more you attend church where the Bible is preached, the more pleasant it becomes.

Your knowledge of Jesus, faith in Him, and your love for Him will grow when you feed on *"the sincere milk of the word"*.

Cops, not Just Bodies in Uniforms

"But when he [Jesus] saw the multitudes, he was moved with compassion on them, because they fainted, and were scattered abroad, as sheep having no shepherd. Then saith he unto his disciples, The harvest truly is plenteous, but the labourers are few; Pray ye therefore the Lord of the harvest, that he will send forth labourers into his harvest." (Matthew 9:36-38)

For some cops, police work is a vocation that deserves their best effort. For others, it's a job. They do it but don't always put much heart into it. For still others, it's little more than a paycheck. They know they'll be paid if they hustle or loaf, so they loaf and let others pull the load.

As a cop, you know who the hustlers and the slugs are on your shift. You have a good idea who'll show up at the next gun run and who won't; whom you can count on for backup, and whom you can't; what bosses care, and what bosses don't.

When an academy class hits the street, it's exciting. A new crew of rookies is all pumped up, eager to do the job and fun to teach. As a 22-year old rookie, I had one field training officer, a big Italian guy named Vince Pendolino. Vince would constantly tell me, "Relax, kid. You're biting at the bit."

Police departments need officers, but not just bodies

in blue uniforms. They need cops who are willing to hustle, inconvenience themselves, take on predators, and help decent people. They need laborers.

Now about our Scripture: Jesus saw young and old, men and women, girls and boys. He saw rich, poor, and middle-class. He saw different cultures and races. He saw white-collar and blue-collar people, refined people and crude, well-educated and not-so-well-educated.

He saw them and had compassion on them. Why? Because for all their differences, they all had one thing in common: they were lost, *"...as sheep having no shepherd."* They needed a Saviour. They needed Jesus.

The greatest thing in the world is to have Jesus as your Saviour. When you have Him, you have eternal life and never need to worry about going to hell: *"He that hath the Son hath life;" (1 John 5:12)*

Yet the worst thing in the world is to be without Christ. A person without Christ is already under condemnation for sin: *"He that believeth on him* [on Jesus] *is not condemned: but he that believeth not is condemned ALREADY* [capitals added]*," (John 3:18)*

The Bible indicates that most people are without Christ. Jesus said, *"...wide is the gate, and broad is the way, that leadeth to destruction, and many there be which go in thereat: Because strait is the gate, and narrow is the way, which leadeth unto life, and few there be that find it." (Matthew 7:13-14)* Isn't that an awful thought? But Jesus said it, so it must be true.

Since it is true, it means that most people you meet are more likely to be lost than saved. That includes citizens, suspects, and even people you work with. That's why the Lord said to pray for LABORERS, people willing to do the actual work of telling lost people about Jesus.

The harvest Jesus spoke about is not a crop of fruit, but of people who need to hear about Jesus. The labourers are believers willing to tell them how Jesus forgives sins and saves souls when people receive Him as Saviour. This work desperately needs laborers today as it did back then.

It's easier for a cop to loaf than to hustle. It's also easier for a Christian not to go out and tell people about Jesus than it is to do so. Yet an officer who won't do his job when he knows that people need his help is doing wrong.

In a much worse way, a Christian who won't try to witness for Christ when he knows that people are headed for hell is also doing wrong. Jesus wants laborers. Lost people need laborers. Pray for laborers and ask the Lord to deal with your heart to be a laborer, as well.

Good Example of a Bad Leader

"...My little finger shall be thicker than my father's loins." (1 Kings 12:10)

Saul was Israel's first king, then David, then David's son Solomon, then Solomon's son Rehoboam. In the last part of Solomon's reign, his fellowship with God went south. He kept company with heathen, ungodly people, and even married heathen wives; all in direct disobedience to God. As a result, *"...his heart was not perfect with the LORD his God," (1 Kings 11:4)*

This is what can happen when you tolerate sin in your life. Sin will harden even a Christian's heart against God. People could surely see by Solomon's life and his reign that he wasn't right with God.

When Solomon died, Rehoboam took over. A group of people led by one Jeroboam, a former servant of Solomon, asked Rehoboam to *"...make thou the grievous service of thy father, and his heavy yoke which he put upon us, lighter, and we will serve thee." (1 Kings 12:4)* Apparently Solomon had imposed some sort of harsh rule on them, and they wanted relief.

Rehoboam asked the older men who had advised his father Solomon how to respond to this request. They told him to speak and act favorably to them, and *"...they will be thy servants for ever." (1 Kings 12:7)*

Unfortunately, Rehoboam ignored this wise advice and asked his young buddies with whom he'd grown up, who knew no more about leadership than he did, what to do.

They advised him to give the people this answer: *"...My little finger shall be thicker than my father's loins. And now whereas my father did lade you with a heavy yoke, I will add to your yoke: my father hath chastised you with whips, but I will chastise you with scorpions." (1 Kings 12:10-11)*

In other words, "If you think my dad was bad, you haven't seen anything yet." Rehoboam gave them this ugly answer. It blew up in his face. Ten tribes of Israel seceded, leaving Rehoboam with only two: Judah and Benjamin. Rehoboam sent a taxman to the other tribes to collect the tribute, and they stoned him to death.

One of the worst things a nation can have is leaders who don't fear God. Sadly, in America we see no shortage of leaders who don't fear the God who is over them. Rehoboam is an example of how not to lead. No doubt he'd gotten lessons in bad leadership from Solomon, but he also made bad decisions on his own. If you're in a leadership position, here are some important lessons:

Lesson One: Leadership--political leadership or police leadership--is a place where God put you: *"...the powers that be are ordained of God." (Romans 13:1)*

So you're not there for you. You're there for God.

Lesson Two: Leadership is a place for you to serve God, not for you and your cronies to abuse the power that God has entrusted you with to make yourselves rich, and to oppress those under you.

Lesson Three: Leadership by oppression-- *"My little finger shall be thicker than my father's loins."*--is no way to lead. It's certainly no way to lead cops.

Cops should strive to be professional, but criminals often fight dirty. Cops know that as they fight criminals, they may violate a rule or two. They also know that if a boss is willing to suspend them on minor rule violations and cost them money, they'll stop hustling, if only for their own financial survival.

If you're a leader who makes things tough on cops, you're also making things tough on decent citizens, and easy on criminals.

Lesson Four: Like with Rehoboam, what you do will come back to you, whether it's good or bad: *"Be not deceived; God is not mocked: for whatsoever a man soweth, that shall he also reap." (Galatians 6:7)*

Moral Courage

"Be strong and of a good courage: for unto this people shalt thou divide for an inheritance the land, which I sware unto their fathers to give them. Only be thou strong and very courageous, that thou mayest observe to do according to all the law, which Moses my servant commanded thee: turn not from it to the right hand or to the left, that thou mayest prosper whithersoever thou goest." (Joshua 1:6-7)

Moses has just died. Joshua is now Israel's leader. During Moses' leadership, God had brought the ten plagues to Egypt, parted the Red Sea, destroyed Egypt's army, kept Israel alive for forty years in the wilderness, and many other miracles.

Joshua would not do what Moses did. Yet God promised Joshua, *"...as I was with Moses, so I will be with thee:"* (Joshua 1:5)

God told Joshua to *"Be strong and of a good courage: for unto this people shalt thou divide for an inheritance the land,"* God knew Israel could be tempted to give in to fear and not go into the promised land because of the fierce people there.

In fact, forty years earlier Israel had done just that. They refused to believe God and revolted against Moses' leadership. As a result, God made them wander forty years in the wilderness until the rebellious people died. God didn't want His people to give in to unbelief again.

God also said, *"Only be thou strong and very courageous, **that thou mayest observe to do according to all the law** [boldface added],...turn not from it to the right hand or to the left, that thou mayest prosper whithersoever thou goest."* Joshua needed to obey God--to do things God's way--in order to have God's blessing. Here is an important lesson: if we want God's blessing, we need to obey Him, even when others don't.

Cops go to dangerous calls and put their lives on the line for each other. That's how they form a strong bond of camaraderie. That's good. Yet the flip side of that bond is peer pressure to go along with others' questionable conduct. This pressure can be especially tough when other officers have seniority or are in a large majority.

Refusing to engage in others' wrongdoing can seem scarier than going to a "shots fired" call. Yet it also requires courage, moral courage. That's the second courage God wanted from Joshua.

You'll no doubt be tempted some time in your career to go along with others' wrongdoing. If you don't, they may gossip about you. They may write about you on the bathroom wall—no signature, of course. Don't let their childish conduct bother you. You've shown moral courage and done what pleases God: *"I know also, my*

God, that thou triest the heart, and hast pleasure in uprightness." (1 Chronicles 29:17)

Given the toxic environment that cops have to work in nowadays, you also need to resist temptation to be lazy because "the people in power don't want you to work." People in power may set policies that help criminals and make life hard for decent people. They may not see the damage their policies do and, quite honestly, they may not care. Yet you see the damage their policies do. That's why, unlike some of them, you need to care about decent citizens. Don't abandon decent citizens to the mercy of criminals.

Bad policy is the sin of the people in power, not yours. Don't "just answer radio" and nothing else because "the people in power don't want you to work." Don't ignore traffic violations or pedestrian stops because there's too much paperwork or because a suspect may fight, and a boss may whine because he has to do a use-of-force investigation.

Do the best work you can within the restrictions you're stuck with and do it honestly. Resist temptation to do wrong, whether temptation comes from other cops or from people in power. That's what God wants. That's moral courage.

Growing Through Exercise

"But refuse profane and old wives' fables, and exercise thyself rather unto godliness. For bodily exercise profiteth little: but godliness is profitable unto all things, having promise of the life that now is, and of that which is to come." (1 Timothy 4:7-8)

The statement, *"...bodily exercise profiteth little:"* doesn't mean exercise is bad. Physical exercise is good. The Christian life is compared to running and boxing- *"I therefore so run, not as uncertainly; so fight I, not as one that beateth the air:" (1 Corinthians 9:26)*

It's also compared to wrestling- *"For we wrestle not against flesh and blood, but against principalities, against powers, against the rulers of the darkness of this world, against spiritual wickedness in high places." (Ephesians 6:12)* Runners, boxers, and wrestlers need to work hard to excel. So, in a way the Bible endorses physical exercise.

Physical exercise also benefits *"little"*; that is, it has some benefit. All else being equal, a Christian in good shape can expect a longer, healthier life of serving the Lord than one who is overweight and unhealthy.

Godly exercise also benefits this life AND the next: *"...godliness is profitable unto all things, having promise of the life that now is, and of that which is to come."*

Pushups, chin-ups, and weights are good for upper body strength. Running and cycling are good for strong legs and aerobic health. Boxing and wrestling help combat endurance.

Upper body strength is good. Upper body strength, a strong heart, and strong legs are better. All these plus combat endurance are better still. As a cop, you never know when you'll need to run, fight, or respond to a dangerous incident.

Unfortunately, some officers let themselves become overweight and out of shape. They are less ready for emergencies, and their health can suffer.

Paul uses physical exercise to explain why spiritual exercise is important for a Christian. Just as you need to exercise to be physically healthy, you need spiritual exercise to be spiritually healthy. So, what exercises can you do to be spiritually healthy?

For one, take time to listen to God's voice as you read His Word. Take time also to speak with Him in prayer. Attend a Bible-preaching church faithfully and be involved in an outreach ministry where you share the gospel with people. These are all areas where Christians should strive— *"exercise"*--to be strong.

Physical exercise takes discipline. At times you may not feel like working out, but you need to fight past the temptation to be lazy and "just do it", as the Nike commercial says. So it is with reading your Bible, prayer, church attendance, or service. You need to fight the devil's temptation and "just do it."

Physical exercise also must be consistent and challenging. You need to exercise regularly with a challenging workout. Results take time and patience, but they do come.

In the same way, don't just read your Bible and pray just to get it over with. Ask the Lord to speak to your heart with His Word and trust Him to do it. Pray like you're talking with Someone who cares about you, because He does. Ask Him to help you grow in your relationship with Him and trust Him to help you.

There should never be a time when you say, "Ok, now I'm fit, so I'll stop exercising." No, fitness is a pattern of life to strive after. Also, as a Christian, you should never say, "Ok, I'm godly now, so I'll stop reading my Bible and praying and attending church." Godliness is not a goal that you reach. It's more a pattern of life to follow as you live your Christian life.

Skeptical, but Honest

"So then faith cometh by hearing, and hearing by the word of God." (Romans 10:17)

Part of your job as a cop is not to trust people. Say you pull over a violator and ask for his license. He says he has one, but not on him. He may not have one, or it may be suspended, or he may have forgotten or misplaced it. So, you get his Social Security number for a status check. You're skeptical, but open to the truth.

What if you're called to a burglary? Your suspect has a black hoodie, blue jeans, tan boots. You arrive and walk up to the house. Suddenly a guy comes out the side door: black hoodie, blue jeans, tan boots. You point your gun—you don't want a bad guy getting the drop on you--and yell "STOP! POLICE!" He raises his hands, but he's on edge. He yells, "I'm working here!"

Is he telling the truth? Maybe. Maybe not. Be skeptical but give him a chance to prove himself. If he says he's Joe Schmo, check his ID. If he says the owner sent him, he should have keys and know the owner's name and phone number. The more questions you ask, the more you'll know if he's telling the truth or not.

This Bible verse is good for skeptics. You might not believe there is a God, and you may think most religions are a racket. Well, if you're skeptical but open to the truth, the best way to have your questions answered is to check out the words of the Bible itself.

Our verse says, *"...faith cometh by hearing, and hearing by the word of God."* The Bible claims to be God's Word. How can I know that, you may ask. Good question. The answer is *Romans 10:17*.

It's like a personal challenge from God: "If you want to have faith in Me, the way to get it is to hear My Word." Take up the challenge. Read out of the Bible. Start with a simple portion, like the gospel of John.

God speaks to our hearts through His Word. He uses His Word to guide us, teach us, comfort us, and sometimes convict us of wrongdoing. Sometimes He deals with us in ways that are unpleasant but necessary.

If you give God's Word an honest look, it will touch your heart. If you'll take heed to it, God will use His word in your heart to generate faith in Him--not just an abstract, "something out there" belief, but a real, personal, soul-saving, life-changing faith in Christ.

It's like your burglary suspect. You wouldn't just arrest him. You'd look like an idiot—and possibly be sued—if he were telling the truth and could have proved it. You check his ID, verify his story, and when you're convinced he's legit, leave him to his work.

If you're skeptical about the Bible, be an honest skeptic. Don't just say, "I don't believe it and I don't want to hear about it!" Give God a chance to prove His Word is true.

The more you check His Word, the more you'll see it's the truth, because *"...faith cometh by hearing, and hearing by the word of God."* If you already know Jesus as Saviour, take time to read and memorize God's word. Doing so will strengthen your faith in Christ. It's the same principle for believers, too: *"...faith cometh by hearing, and hearing by the word of God."*

Being Thankful

"Enter into his gates with thanksgiving, and into his courts with praise: be thankful unto him, and bless his name." (Psalm 100:4)

You're on patrol. If a guy asked for change and you bought him some food (how many times have cops done things like this?), what would you think if he just took it without saying "thank you"?

Luke 6:35 says God is *"...kind unto the unthankful and to the evil."* God gives good health to people who don't thank Him. He gives daily blessings to people who deny that He exists or try to malign his character.

Psalm 107:1 says *"O give thanks unto the LORD, for he is good:"* Just as you want a "thank you" when you show kindness, God wants and deserves to hear "thank you" when He shows us kindness.

God shows us kindness every day. *Lamentations 3:22-23* says of God, that *"...his compassions fail not.* **They are new every morning:** *great is thy faithfulness."* [boldface added] *Psalm 68:19* also says, *"Blessed be the Lord, who **daily** [boldface added] loadeth us with benefits, even the God of our salvation. Selah."*

Our passage tells us to enter into God's presence, to *"Enter into his gates..."* and *"...into his courts..."*

How do we do that? God is in heaven. We're on earth.

Still, He sees and hears us. *Psalm 139:7* says, *"Whither shall I go from thy spirit? or whither shall I flee from thy presence?"* God knows what we say and do and even think: *"...I know the things that come into your mind, every one of them." (Ezekiel 11:5)*

When we know Jesus as Saviour, we can *"Enter into his gates **with thanksgiving**,"* and *"...into his courts **with praise:**"* The very next words are, *"**be thankful unto him,**"* [boldfaces added] So we can fellowship with God by thanking Him for what He does for us. *Psalm 22:3* says God *"...inhabitest the praises of Israel."* There's a special sense of God's presence when we take time to thank and praise Him.

Ever ask someone, "How's it going?" and get this reply: "Can't complain. No one listens anyway"? Don't grumble. Be thankful for things God has given you, even simple things like life, health, food, and a home.

James 1:17 says, *"Every good gift and every perfect gift is from above,"* We have many things other people don't. They're gifts from God. Thank Him for them.

Do you love police work? Forget the problems, do you love the job? How many people, do you think, hate their job and would love to do what you do? If you love the job, then thank the Lord for letting you be a cop.

Are you healthy? Are your kids healthy? Next time you see an ad for St. Jude Children's Research Hospital and the worst thing your kids have is a bad attitude now and then (don't we all?) tell the Lord, "Thank you."

Are you in a country where people can speak freely? Where the Bible is available without fear of arrest? If you're not in some oppressive Communist or Third World nation, thank Him for that.

About 1971, a book came out entitled, "Teens Ask Questions," a Dear Abby-type advice book with Q and A given by teenagers. One entry read like this: "My brother is in the Army. When he comes home, I'm glad to see him, but sometimes he bosses me around. What can I do?" One of the answers stuck out: "I wish I had your problem. My brother's in Vietnam."

How many close calls have you had on the job? They weren't luck. They were God's hand. *Nahum 1:3* says, *"...the LORD hath his way in the whirlwind and in the storm,"* Even in a tornado or hurricane, nothing happens that God doesn't control. Don't ever be embarrassed to say, "thank you, Lord" for things that happen on the job.

Do you know Jesus as your Saviour? If so, you have a Saviour who'll never leave you, a Bible to guide you, and an eternal home in heaven to look forward to. Be thankful that you're saved.

Growing Through Storms

"And straightway Jesus constrained his disciples to get into a ship, and to go before him unto the other side, while he sent the multitudes away. And when he had sent the multitudes away, he went up into a mountain apart to pray: and when the evening was come, he was there alone. But the ship was now in the midst of the sea, tossed with waves: for the wind was contrary. And in the fourth watch of the night Jesus went unto them, walking on the sea. And when the disciples saw him walking on the sea, they were troubled, saying, It is a spirit; and they cried out for fear. But straightway Jesus spake unto them, saying, Be of good cheer; it is I; be not afraid. And Peter answered him and said, Lord, if it be thou, bid me come unto thee on the water. And he said, Come. And when Peter was come down out of the ship, he walked on the water, to go to Jesus. But when he saw the wind boisterous, he was afraid; and beginning to sink, he cried, saying, Lord, save me. And immediately Jesus stretched forth his hand, and caught him, and said unto him, O thou of little faith, wherefore didst thou doubt? And when they were come into the ship, the wind ceased." (Matthew 14:22-32)

The disciples are on a ship. It's night. They're fighting a storm. Waves are tossing the ship about. Suddenly the men see someone walking on the sea. Now they're really scared. "It's a spirit!"

It's not a spirit. It's the Lord. Jesus assures them that

it's He. He calms their fear. Here's an important point right here: Jesus has a way of calming our fears with His presence and His Word.

Then Peter gives the Lord a challenge. He says that if it's really Jesus, then He should bid Peter come out and walk on the water, too. A little bold of Peter, maybe?

Interestingly, the Lord wasn't offended at that request. He invited Peter to walk on water, and Peter did. In fact, Peter did fine--until he got his eyes off Jesus and focused on the storm: *"But when he saw the wind boisterous, he was afraid;"* When Peter took his focus off Jesus and onto the storm, his faith wavered and he started to sink.

This story has several great lessons. We see that Jesus sends His followers off, knowing they're headed into a storm. When it hits, He's with them even if they don't realize it.

Lesson 1: If you know Jesus as Saviour, He's always with you, even in the storm. He said, *"...I will never leave thee, nor forsake thee." (Hebrews 13:5)* "Never" means exactly that: Never. Also, *"God is our refuge and strength, a very present help in trouble." (Psalm 46:1)* It doesn't say we won't have trouble. In fact, it says that we *will*, but when we do, God will be present with us.

Lesson 2: He may allow trouble in your life to remind

you of your need for Him: *"In the day of my trouble I sought the Lord:" (Psalm 77:2)*

If things are going well, you may let your Bible reading and prayer time slip, but when trouble comes, you may find yourself reading God's Word and praying more intensely. God has ways to remind us to do that.

With Jesus' help, Peter did what he couldn't do on his own, which brings us to Lesson 3: When you know Jesus as Saviour, He'll help you do what you can't do on your own. Not that you'll walk on water, but He'll give you grace to live for Him, even on this job.

You may think, "I can't be a witness for Jesus as a cop." Yes, you can. *Philippians 4:13* says, *"I can do all things through Christ which strengtheneth me."* You can take that promise, then, and trust God to be good for His Word.

Lesson 4 is from another time when Jesus was with His disciples on a ship and calmed a storm: *"But the men marvelled, saying, What manner of man is this, that even the winds and the sea obey him!" (Matthew 8:27)* Once they saw how the Lord had gotten them through a storm, they knew Him better than they did before and were even more impressed with His greatness.

You'll go through storms as a cop that most people won't. But you'll never go through a storm the Lord can't help you through.

When the Lord gets you through a storm, you're going to know Him better than you did before the storm, and you'll be even more impressed with what a great Saviour and Lord He is! When a storm hits, then, do what the Lord says to do in *Psalm 50:15--"And call upon me in the day of trouble: I will deliver thee, and thou shalt glorify me."*

Healing a Cop's Broken Heart

"He [God] healeth the broken in heart, and bindeth up their wounds." (Psalm 147:3)

As a cop, you often have to act differently from most people. Say a guy mouths off to you on the street. He knows you can't arrest him for just talking. That's why he's doing it.

Now if you arrested him and had to use force, which would probably happen, you'd have to make a long report and your department may suspend you for violating some rule just because that's what they do. Sometimes it's easier to ignore him until he eventually goes away.

Some things on the job are just annoying. Others are more troublesome. Like violent crime. To most people, it's just a story on the news, like sports, weather, or Hollywood gossip. *"Two people were shot to death on Cleveland's near West Side. Police are on scene. And now, big news about ... THE TRIBE!"* But violent crime is reality for decent people in tough neighborhoods and for cops trying to help them.

You fly lights-and-sirens to a scene, heart racing. Doors are kicked in, houses torn up, crying victims. And dead bodies. Staring lifelessly. Blood, guts, brain matter. It's horrible. Sometimes they're kids. Then it's really horrible. You see things you don't forget. You search for suspects, your gun in your hand and your heart in your throat. That's violent crime.

Then there are roach-infested houses, abused kids, liberal justice, personnel shortages, toxic media, micromanagement, talking heads who have never done your job, lack of political support, and punitive leadership, just to name a few.

Police work is an important job, but it can be troubling and depressing. You learn to put on a professional face, but some things on the job trouble you and some will break your heart, besides whatever personal problems you may have.

Well, God knows all about it: *"...he knoweth the secrets of the heart." (Psalm 44:21)* This doesn't just mean God knows if you're thinking sinful thoughts, although it does mean that. It also means God knows what troubles you. You don't need to explain anything to Him. Some things you can discuss with other cops but not with outsiders. They wouldn't understand. But God is not an outsider. He understands.

Our opening verse also says God heals the broken-hearted and binds up their wounds. Cops can have broken hearts that need to be healed like anyone else. Why else is this job so plagued by divorce, alcoholism, and suicide? God can heal everybody else's broken hearts. He can heal cops' broken hearts, too.

One way that God heals broken hearts is with His Word: *"He sent his word, and healed them," (Psalm 107:20)* The Bible is not just a big book of "Thou shalts" and "Thou shalt nots." The book of Psalms, for instance, is God's Word but it's also the expressions of a man's heart.

David wrote many psalms. Some of his work he wrote when he was deeply troubled and unhappy. As you read in Psalms, don't be surprised to find a passage that encourages your heart in a personal way. That's what God does through His Word.

The Bible is a powerful book like no other. God uses it to minister to hurting hearts. Most of all, the Bible tells us how to be sure of a home in heaven.

Too Crazy!

"And there was a great famine in Samaria: and, behold, they besieged it, until an ass's head was sold for fourscore pieces of silver, and the fourth part of a cab of dove's dung for five pieces of silver.

And as the king of Israel was passing by upon the wall, there cried a woman unto him, saying, Help, my lord, O king. And he said, If the LORD do not help thee, whence shall I help thee? out of the barnfloor, or out of the winepress? And the king said unto her, What aileth thee? And she answered, This woman said unto me, Give thy son, that we may eat him to-day, and we will eat my son to-morrow.

So we boiled my son, and did eat him: and I said unto her on the next day, Give thy son, that we may eat him: and she hath hid her son." (2 Kings 6:25-29)

You've probably dealt with crazy stuff on the job, but anything like this? Say the dispatcher gives you this assignment: "5 Adam 13, I have a call of…two women…uh, arguing...about a child... that's been… BOILED??" She's reading off the computer screen. You can hear the disbelief in her voice.

When you arrive, you meet Mary. She tells you her neighbor, Sue, talked her into boiling her son so they could eat him. Sue said they'd eat her son the next day, but then she went back on her word.

Obviously, Mary doesn't care about either kid. She

just wants what she thinks is fair. What do you do, other than call for a boss?

Apparently, it wasn't a crime at that time to kill and boil your kid. In fact, child sacrifice had been practiced in heathen nations, and Israel picked it up. This was one reason God had warned Israel not to mingle with the heathen when they entered Canaan. They didn't listen:

"They [the Israelites] *did not destroy the nations, concerning whom the LORD commanded them:*
But were mingled among the heathen, and learned their works. And they served their idols: which were a snare unto them. Yea, they sacrificed their sons and their daughters unto devils, And shed innocent blood, even the blood of their sons and of their daughters, whom they sacrificed unto the idols of Canaan: and the land was polluted with blood." (Psalm 106:34-38)

The king knew God had sent the famine: *"And he said, If the LORD do not help thee, whence shall I help thee? out of the barnfloor, or out of the winepress?"* But he didn't seem to care WHY God had sent it, or about helping Israel recover spiritually.

In fact, his heart seemed hardened against God. Sin does that. It hardens hearts against God. *Hebrews 3:13* warns us, *"...lest any of you be hardened through the deceitfulness of sin."* The king was also ready to take out his anger on God's man: *"God do so and more also to me, if the head of Elisha the son of Shaphat shall stand on him this day." (2 Kings 6:31)*

It was a time when God chastised Israel severely for turning against Him. Yet God also blessed those who wanted to do right and please Him.

Not far from this story, we read of a preacher's widow and her two young sons who were in debt. The creditor was going to take the boys as servants, but God provided funds for them miraculously by means of a pot of oil.

We also read of a well-to-do lady and her husband who had an extra room built for Elisha to lodge in. God blessed their generosity and gave them a child. We also read of a brave but prideful Syrian army captain named Naaman who had leprosy. He dipped into the Jordan river seven times, was cured of his leprosy, and became a worshipper of the true God, the God of Israel.

As a cop, you see vile, wicked things that most people never see and that you may never talk about, besides to other cops. That's beside the everyday sin that all of us see and hear. But all that sin doesn't have to dominate your life if you don't want it to. God can give you grace and help to live happy and pleasing to Him and enjoy fellowship and service with Him, regardless what others do or how sinful the culture gets.

Growing Through Service

"That we henceforth be no more children, tossed to and fro, and carried about with every wind of doctrine, by the sleight of men, and cunning craftiness, whereby they lie in wait to deceive; But speaking the truth in love, may grow up into him [Christ] *in all things,"* (Ephesians 4:14-15)

Newborn babies are great, but they shouldn't stay babies. They need to grow. In the same way, once you receive Jesus as your Saviour and are born again, you need to grow as a Christian. That's what this passage is talking about: *"That we* [believers in Jesus] *henceforth be no more children* [spiritually immature], *"*

Kids need guidance. As a cop, you've probably seen dysfunctional, fractured homes where kids don't get good guidance. I was on church visitation once at a home. The young woman at the house had her son sipping beer. He was about five years old. She said she'd heard that if kids get alcohol when they're young they won't have a taste for it later. Where in the world did she hear that?

Christians also need guidance from the Bible to help them grow in their Christian faith. Our passage also warns against being *"...carried about with every wind of doctrine,"* which is wrong religious doctrine, and there's no shortage of that. The Bible is our guide to help us discern good religious doctrine from bad.

Our passage also talks about growth through service: *"But **speaking the truth in love** [boldface added], may grow up..."* This passage, *"speaking the truth in love,"* refers to telling others about Jesus. The Lord Himself commanded, *"Go ye into all the world, and preach the gospel to every creature." (Mark 16:15)*

Witnessing should be part of every Christian's life. It's also an important part of Christian growth. A Christian may read his Bible, pray, and attend church, but if he never tells others about Jesus, he's disobeying Christ and missing a vital part of his Christian life.

To illustrate the point: a kid may eat well and study hard, but if he never learns to work; to mow the lawn, rake leaves, shovel snow, help around the house, or work a job, what is he actually accomplishing?

Witnessing is also like police work, in a way. As a cop, you learn laws, tactics, and rules of evidence. But it's not just about knowing what to do. You need to apply the knowledge. Don't be like some cops who know a lot but don't apply their knowledge. They may do well on promotional tests and make rank, but then they can become bosses who don't do much police work. Knowledge isn't helpful if you won't use it.

Here's another thought: if you're saved, you probably remember who first told you about Jesus. If you grew up in a Christian home, it may have been a parent. If not, maybe it was a friend or co-worker. The point is that God didn't appear to you in a vision or send an angel to tell you about Jesus. Some human being was used of God to reach you with the gospel.

Likewise, God wants you to be willing to be used of Him to reach others with the gospel. Witnessing to people is an important and exciting part of Christian growth.

Being saved is something to be glad about, but it isn't just about being glad you're saved. The Lord wants us to tell others about Him, just as someone told us. Imagine a cop saying he's glad he's a cop, but he never does much police work (maybe you know some cops like that). It's good he's glad to be a cop, but he's on the job to serve.

As Christians we're also here to serve the Lord and tell others about Him. Serving is an important part of growth as a Christian.

Playing on an Unlevel Field

"...as concerning this sect, we know that every where it is spoken against." (Acts 28:22)

Before his conversion, Saul of Tarsus was a strict Jew and persecuted Christians horribly. One day as he was on the road to Damascus, the Lord dealt with him. He received Jesus as Saviour and was powerfully used of God to reach people with the gospel.

Later known as Paul, he used his Scripture knowledge to explain to people in the synagogues how Jesus fulfilled Old Testament prophecies about the Messiah. Many Jews didn't want to hear that, and had him arrested, trying to discredit and destroy him.

Paul was a Roman citizen and appealed to Caesar against them. When he arrived at Rome, he met with Jewish leaders there. One of them told Paul, *"...every where it* [Christianity] *is spoken against."* What had the early Christians done or said that was so offensive, that their religion was bad-mouthed so much?

Quite possibly it was nothing, but the fake news put out by their enemies was so viral that it may have been the only thing people heard, if no one took the time to learn the truth. The Christians were playing on an unlevel field.

As a cop, you're often not on a level playing field.

Activists, protesters and other talking heads get face time bad-mouthing cops, yet have they ever worked a police car in a high-crime neighborhood? Or spoken with a victim of violent crime? When criminals and their sympathizers get face time, politicians get uptight, cops get cuffed, and decent people in tough areas don't get good police work. Such is the nature of the job.

You often can't respond to accusations, and the citizens who support you don't want to be on TV for the criminals. As a result, people may often get only one side of the story about a police-related incident.

One evening around autumn 1985, Andy Gonzalez and I had just dropped off a prisoner downtown and were back on patrol. Andy turned onto Auburn Avenue and asked if I wanted to stop for coffee. I replied, "Nah, let's see what kind of trouble we can get into."

Just as those words came out of my mouth, Andy reached the corner of Auburn and Scranton. We looked to our right and saw a 13-year old kid drop from the fire escape of a building onto the sidewalk. The building was a business, and it was closed. We figured he'd tried to break into the building.

When he saw us, his eyes bugged out like deer in the headlights. He took off running. I bailed out of the car and ran after him. Andy wheeled the car around. The kid ran south on Scranton, then into a school yard. Andy pulled up, jumped the curb with the car, and knocked a tire off the rim, flattening it. He jumped out, caught the kid, and we put him into the car.

We took him back to the business he'd tried to break into, or that we *thought* he'd tried to break into. As it turned out, the access door was sealed, so he couldn't have gotten in if he'd tried, and we had no proof that he'd tried.

He'd probably climbed onto the fire escape because 13-year-olds do things like that. Yet one of his buddies had told him that if the police saw him up there, they'd shoot him. He got down just as we pulled up. What do you think was going through his mind when he saw us?

He obviously thought we'd shoot him. Who knows how often fake news comes out about the police from people who have no idea what they're talking about?

Andy and I thought he was breaking in. He thought he was about to be shot. All three of us acted in good faith, but on bad info. In the end, we let the kid go.

You can't stop the anti-police rumor mill or fake news, but you can do your job in a way that discredits it. So it is with the Christian faith. You can't stop the fake news, but you can trust the Lord to give you grace to live above it and share Christ's love with people. He will, no matter how unlevel the playing field is.

Street-Smarts

"Behold, I send you forth as sheep in the midst of wolves: be ye therefore wise as serpents, and harmless as doves." (Matthew 10:16)

Most people who complain about police have never dealt with a violent criminal on the level you have. They don't see how brutal criminals can be and what they're willing to do. You need to know how criminals think so they'll be less equipped to hurt you or the citizens you're sworn to protect.

In 1991, Texas Constable Darrell Lunsford pulled over three young Hispanic men hauling a large quantity of marijuana. As Lunsford and two of the suspects stood at the trunk of the car talking, one of them told one of his buddies in Spanish (which Lunsford didn't understand) that they would have to kill Lunsford.

The two suspects jumped Lunsford. The third exited the car and joined the other two. They beat and kicked Lunsford, stabbed him, and shot him to death with his own weapon (info taken from PoliceOne.Com/Topics/Officer Down). The whole incident was caught on Lunsford's car video camera.

You can look up the name "Darrell Lunsford" on the internet and watch the video. It's sickening because you already know what's about to happen. Yet it has some important tactical lessons. Lesson One: don't be reluctant to call for backup. Lunsford was alone at the time, and even though he was much larger than his assailants, he was also much older at age 47 and still up against two extra sets of arms and legs.

Lesson Two: NEVER let suspicious people talk with each other in a language you can't understand, especially if you're outnumbered. You don't know what they're saying. If you don't have someone you trust who speaks the language, tell them to speak English. If they won't, you could be in serious danger.

The Lord wasn't talking about police work in this verse, but it does have important application to witnessing for Christ. Witnessing isn't often easy. That's why the Lord said to be "wise as serpents"—clever or "streetwise" in our approach—and at the same time "harmless as doves", since we don't want to hurt or offend people. Far from it. We want to share the greatest news they'll ever hear.

Witnessing may be tough, though, for several reasons, such as: 1) You're intruding into people's lives, and sometimes onto their property, uninvited; and 2) You're telling them something they may not feel like hearing. Don't be surprised, then, when you run into obstacles.

Some people have had bad experiences with "religious" people. Others may think "religion" is all a racket, or that born-again Christians are the same as

Jehovah's Witnesses or Mormons. In order to overcome any possible barriers, you need a smart, streetwise approach.

If you want to affect others for Christ, be kind and gracious. *Colossians 3:12* says, *"Put on therefore, as the elect of God, holy and beloved, bowels of mercies, kindness, humbleness of mind, meekness, longsuffering;"* It's been said that if you want to win people to Christ, you have to win them to yourself.

Be kind and helpful, then ask the Lord to give you an opening to share a tract that tells people from the Bible how to be saved. Trust God to answer the prayer. He wants people saved much more than we do.

Once the Lord opens the door, give someone the tract and invite him to church. If you go to a church where people hear how to be saved (why go to any other kind?), you could have your church's info on the tract.

If he takes it, even if you've gotten no farther than that, you've given him some Scripture to think about and for the Lord to use to work on his heart. Ask the Lord to convict him of his need to receive Christ. You've "planted a seed" and done so wisely, as the Lord said to do.

Growing in a Good Environment

"Blessed is the man that walketh not in the counsel of the ungodly, nor standeth in the way of sinners, nor sitteth in the seat of the scornful. But his delight is in the law of the LORD;" (Psalm 1:1-2)

As a cop, you may have handled domestics where the residence is filthy and bug-infested, the two live-in combatants are screaming obscenities at each other, alcohol is lying about, and the shelves are stocked with dirty, violent movies and music.

Then you see small kids there and you may wonder, "What chance do they have in this environment? Will they end up just like the parents?"

Of course, a bad environment could also be a posh house in the suburbs, where Mom and Dad are too busy making money to teach their kids about God or pay them attention or show them love. They just give them money and send them to the mall.

Your environment is what influences you. You can't usually help what comes into your environment at work. You can't stop other cops from talking dirty, telling crude jokes or gossiping. You'll also deal all day long with people who don't talk right, dress right, or act right. That's part of the job. You can't choose the calls you handle.

If you're called to, say, a child rape victim, you can't refuse to go. Yes, it's disgusting, but you're the police. You need to deal with it.

You also can't ignore a "shots fired" or "robbery in progress" call because of the danger. If you know Jesus as Saviour, you'd better not ignore it! Other cops fly to calls like those all the time, and many of them are unsaved. What a disgrace it would be for a child of God to refuse to go to a run like that!

Aside from the job, though, you CAN choose most of what goes into your heart through your eyes and ears. *Lamentations 3:51* says, *"Mine eye affecteth mine heart..."* which means that what you see—and what you hear—affects your heart.

That's why our verse says not to walk *"...in the counsel of the ungodly,"* stand *"...in the way of sinners,"* or sit *"...in the seat of the scornful."* In short, don't let ungodly people influence you. God even says, *"Blessed is the man..."* who won't do that.

So how do you avoid influences of ungodly people? One way is not to spend too much time with ungodly people on the job. If other officers like to talk filthy or gossip or backbite, don't spend time in their conversations.

Another is to consider how you entertain yourself. Do you watch TV shows or movies where the actors use foul language, tell vile jokes, or dress indecently? Do they glorify or make light of sin? TV and movie producers are in it for money. Their concern--or lack of it--about pleasing God is evident in the show's content.

So, if a program is trashy, displeasing to God, and not good for a Christian to watch (not that it's good for anyone else, either), why watch it? The same could be said for what you hear on the radio. The Bible has no *"Thou shalt not"* against secular radio or TV shows, but are you feeding yourself spiritual poison as you're being entertained or informed?

For a good spiritual environment, you also need to be in a Bible-believing church where salvation is preached and that reaches out to people with the gospel. That's part of the point of *"But his delight is in the law of the LORD;"* At a church like this, you can learn to love God's Word.

You'll be challenged in your Christian life when you hear His Word preached and taught. You'll learn more about Jesus and about serving Him. You'll also meet people who can help and encourage you to grow in your Christian life.

Honesty with Kindness

"...speaking the truth in love," (Ephesians 4:15)

You don't have to be a cop to know that we live in a sinful world. Sin is everywhere. In this sinful, spiritually dark world, Jesus commanded us, *"Let your light so shine before men," (Matthew 5:16)*

When you do a traffic stop in the daytime, you may not use a flashlight, at least not at first. At night, though, you *need* a flashlight to see what a violator may be trying to hide—or pull out to use against you. The darker it is, the more a bright light helps. In this sinful, dark world, God wants His people to share Christ's love and grace, to *"Let your light so shine before men,"*

Did someone ever walk into a room where you were asleep and flip on a light? The sudden flash of light was irritating, but if you had to get up, it helped you. In the same way, that's what the Bible does in people's lives.

People can be irritated to hear the light of God's Word spoken against the darkness of their sin. *John 3:19* says, *"...light is come into the world, and men loved darkness rather than light, because their deeds were evil."*

Yet the Holy Spirit uses God's Word to show lost people their need to repent of sin and receive Jesus as Saviour. When they receive Jesus, they're glad that someone shared the light of the gospel with them.

We live in a time when *"...truth is fallen in the street," (Isaiah 59:14)* People may not want to hear the truth because it's politically incorrect, or they simply enjoy their sin. Still, the truth needs to be told, but kindly.

Not speaking the truth to people who need to hear it is unkind. If a man has cancer, the worst thing his doctor could do is not tell him. In the same way, the worst thing a Christian could do to needy sinners is not tell them that their sins have separated them from a holy God and condemned them to hell. If people don't hear the truth about their sin, they won't hear how Jesus can save them. People need to hear the truth.

People need to hear the truth about sin: about dishonesty--*"Thou shalt not bear false witness..." (Exodus 20:16);* about alcohol--*"Wine is a mocker, strong drink is raging:" (Proverbs 20:1)*; about pornography-- *"I will set no wicked thing before mine eyes:" (Psalm 101:3)*; about profanity--*"Let no corrupt communication proceed out of your mouth," (Ephesians 4:29)*; about gambling--*"He that hasteth to be rich hath an evil eye," (Proverbs 28:22)*, and other sins that make people wrong with God and wreck lives.

People involved in same-sex intimacy or "transgender" behavior need to hear God's truth against their sin: *"Thou shalt not lie with mankind, as* with womankind:" (Leviticus 18:22) "The woman shall not wear that which pertaineth unto a man, neither shall a man put on a woman's garment:" (Deuteronomy 22:5) They need to hear the truth, but they need to hear it in a kind way.

Mark 2:15 says, "...many publicans and sinners sat also together with Jesus..." These people knew what they were guilty of. No doubt Jesus was honest with them about their sin. He told the woman living in adultery, "For thou hast had five husbands; and he whom thou now hast is not thy husband:" (John 4:18)

Yet He also cared about them and offered forgiveness for their sins. Christians don't speak of people's sins because we hate them, but because God loves them and wants them to have forgiveness of sins by receiving Jesus as their Saviour, too.

It was said of Jesus, "This man receiveth sinners," (Luke 15:2), and it's still true. Jesus died for sins, was buried, rose again, and today still receives and saves sinners who come to Him today. That's why it's so important for us who know Him as Saviour to be "...speaking the truth in love,"

High-Performance Spiritual Food

"But he [Jesus] *answered and said, It is written, Man shall not live by bread alone, but by every word that proceedeth out of the mouth of God." (Matthew 4:4)*

As Jesus fasted in the wilderness, the devil tempted Him to use His power as God to turn stones to bread: *"And when the tempter came to him, he said, If thou be the Son of God, command that these stones be made bread." (Matthew 4:3)*

Jesus could have used His power as God to order the devil to be gone and the devil would have had to obey. Of course, that wouldn't help us when we're tempted since we're not God the Son and we don't have that divine power. Instead, He used a weapon we can also use—Scripture.

Here's a lesson from this verse: if you're saved but tempted to sin, take a Scripture that deals with that sin and quote it--out loud, if need be. Sound crazy? It helps. That's what Jesus did: *"For the word of God is quick, and powerful, and sharper than any two-edged sword," (Hebrews 4:12)* God's Word helps us to resist temptation: *"Thy word have I hid in mine heart, that I might not sin against thee." (Psalm 119:11)*

We need good food daily--and enough of it, not just a bite here and there—to be healthy and strong. It's the same way with Scripture. We need to feed ourselves with the spiritual food of God's Word.

What do you feed your mind and spirit with throughout the day? Some people may feed on Facebook, spending who-knows-how-much-time reading and replying to other people's posts.

Others feed on talk radio. They love to hear Joe Bigmouth (fictitious) say, "Let's go to Bob in Cleveland, Ohio. Bob, you're on the Joe Bigmouth show." And Bob (also fictitious) starts out with, "Thanks, Joe, for taking my call. It's such an honor to talk with you..."

Really? An honor? Joe may be politically/socially conservative and pro-police, but if he has no testimony for Christ, and if he has a dirty mouth (which indicates a dirty heart, because *"...out of the abundance of the heart the mouth speaketh." Matthew 12:34)*, don't count on him for spiritual nourishment.

As for Facebook, it can be helpful, but it can also be a time waster. Some posts may be helpful, but others may just be gossipy and not worth reading. Ever hear people say, "I don't do Facebook"? That may be why.

If you're saved, God's Word should be the biggest influence in your life. *Psalm 119:105* says, *"Thy word is a lamp unto my feet, and a light unto my path."* If you're walking through a dark place, you keep the light on the whole time to guide your every step. In the same way, God's Word is a guide for each step of our lives.

The more you hide its words in your heart, the stronger you get. *"...I have written unto you, young men, **because ye are strong, and the word of God abideth in you**, and ye have overcome the wicked one* [boldface added]. " *(1 John 2:14)* When you memorize and recite Scripture, you can also enjoy it without a Bible in front of you. Scripture memorizing also helps you to develop a good memory, which is important for a police officer to have.

Feed on God's Word often. Find passages that you enjoy and memorize them. Bible memorizing is like exercise. The more you do, the stronger you get. The stronger you get, the more you enjoy it. The more you enjoy it, the more you do, and you enjoy God's Word more than those who just read it now and then.

When you feed on God's Word by reading it and thinking about what you've memorized, the Lord uses it to help you in your walk with Him.

Watch out for Impostors

"Take heed that no man deceive you. For many shall come in my name, saying, I am Christ; and shall deceive many." (Matthew 24:4-5)

As Jesus described troubles that would come in the last days, He gave this warning. He knew His name would be a household word long after He was gone. He warned that many deceivers would come along claiming to be Him.

We also see His prophecy has come true. Look at how many religions mention the name of Jesus Christ. The problem is that the Jesus Christ of many religions is not the same as the Jesus Christ of the Bible. They're false Christs. The Lord warned: *"For there shall arise false Christs, and false prophets," (Matthew 24:24)*

Some may say, "Well, it's all the same Jesus. Others just believe different things about Him." No, it's not all the same Jesus. The religious doctrine about them may contain some Bible truth, but it also has the religion's false doctrine because the other Christs are literally impostors.

Say you get John Smith on a traffic stop. You run a warrant check and get a hit. Do you arrest him? With a name like John Smith, you'd better check the physical description, date of birth, and SS number so you don't arrest the wrong guy.

The Bible also gives us no shortage of info to know the true Jesus Christ from a false Christ. For one, the true Jesus Christ is God, every bit as much as God the Father is God. *John 1:1* says, *"In the beginning was the Word, and the Word was with God, and the Word was God."* This certain person was known as "the Word." That person was Jesus, and He was God.

John 1:14 also says, *"And the Word was made flesh, and dwelt among us,"* So Jesus, who is *"the Word"*, was God and flesh at the same time. *1 John 3:16* also says, *"Hereby perceive we the love of God, because he laid down his life for us:"* The God who *"laid down his life for us"* is the Jesus Christ of the Bible.

In Mormon, Jehovah's Witnesses', and Islamic doctrine, Jesus Christ is not God. They may call Him a lesser god or a prophet, but the Christ of these religions is a false Christ, which makes them false religions.

Jesus' Deity (Godhood) is important. Some may say He was just a great moral teacher, but He laid claim to being God when He said, *"I and my Father are one."* *(John 10:30)* So either He was God or He wasn't.

If He wasn't, then He lied. If He lied, then He wasn't even a great moral teacher. He was a liar and blasphemer (which the religious leaders accused Him of being), and His death on the cross was just the death of a sinner and did nothing to pay our sin-debt.

Yet He rose again, and *"...was seen of above five hundred brethren at once;" (1 Corinthians 15:6),* which proved that His claim to being God and dying to forgive us our sins is true. A liar and sinner wouldn't have risen from the dead.

Being God, the true Jesus can also do something only God can do: forgive sins. Jesus once told a lame man, *"Son, thy sins be forgiven thee." (Mark 2:5)* The religious leaders hit the roof when they heard that. They said, *"Why doth this man thus speak blasphemies? who can forgive sins but God only?" (Mark 2:7)*

That was just the point. Jesus knew what He was saying. Only God can forgive sins, and since Jesus is God, He could forgive sins. To prove His point, He also healed the lame man, something else that only God could do.

The true Jesus also saves repentant sinners by His grace who come to Him to be saved. Some may say that going to heaven is a matter of doing good or having religion. Not true. Jesus said that He is the only way to heaven: *"I am the way, the truth, and the life: no man cometh unto the Father, but by me." (John 14:6)*

The true Jesus Christ forgives sins, saves souls and gives eternal life by His grace, but a false Christ is deceptive, as our passage says, and can do nothing. Don't believe they're all the same. They're not.

No Time for a Break

"And the apostles gathered themselves together unto Jesus, and told him all things, both what they had done, and what they had taught. And he said unto them, Come ye yourselves apart into a desert place, and rest a while: for there were many coming and going, and they had no leisure so much as to eat. And they departed into a desert place by ship privately. And the people saw them departing, and many knew him, and ran afoot thither out of all cities, and outwent them, and came together unto him. And Jesus, when he came out, saw much people, and was moved with compassion toward them, because they were as sheep not having a shepherd: and he began to teach them many things." (Mark 6:30-34)

Jesus and His disciples had been busy ministering; so busy, in fact, that they hadn't had time to eat. The Lord saw the disciples could use a rest and told them to go to a desert place. People saw them leaving and wanted to see Jesus and hear what He had to say. Somehow they learned where His ship would land.

As they went to the place, others may have seen them and asked where they were headed. Word got around that they were going to see Jesus. The crowd apparently grew larger and larger: men and women, old and young. When the ship finally landed, the Lord didn't see a quiet place to rest. Instead He saw a big crowd who wanted to see Him. He may have been tired and hungry Himself, but He put the break on hold.

Ever work one of those shifts that are almost nonstop? The dispatcher gives out stacks of runs and every so often she'll say, "Any car able to break off,…" About the time you think the board is clear and you ask for lunch, she may say, "I just got a domestic call in, can you handle it?" Sorry, no break. If you've ever worked a shift like that, you have an idea what the Lord and the disciples were going through.

The Lord didn't get angry because these people showed up. He *"…was moved with compassion toward them,"* It's also interesting to note *why* He had compassion toward them. The Scripture doesn't say that any of them were ill, had lost a loved one, were hungry, troubled by demons, or any other problems, although Jesus had dealt with many different problems, including these. We have no reason to think these people weren't healthy and functional.

So why did they need compassion? *"…because they were as sheep not having a shepherd:"* They had no one to tell them the truth about a God who loved them. No one to care about their souls. No one to guide them. No one to give them words of hope for eternity. But now Jesus was there, *"…and he began to teach them many things."*

The passage doesn't tell us exactly what Jesus told them. But we can look elsewhere in Scripture and see things Jesus said. Jesus spoke words of compassion, love, hope, and most importantly, truth. Jesus even said, *"I am the way, the TRUTH, and the life:" (John 14:6, capitals added)*

Jesus spoke words of compassion and hope, of sins forgiven and an eternal home in heaven. He also spoke words of purpose, of sharing His truth and His love with others. People could trust Jesus' words because they came from God in the flesh, and God cannot lie.

Nice story, but what does it have to do with you, right? It has everything to do with you. Jesus loves you as much as He loved those people. You can't see, hear, or touch Him like they did, but He died for your sins, was buried, rose again, and is alive!

"I am he that LIVETH, and WAS dead; and, behold, I AM ALIVE FOR EVERMORE, Amen;" (Revelation 1:18, capitals added)

He still forgives sins, saves souls, and changes lives. His Word speaks to hearts today as powerfully as ever.

As a cop, you have an important purpose: mainly to help decent people against predators. But where is your hope beyond that? What do you hope for, besides to make it to retirement? Jesus wants to give you a sure hope for eternity and a purpose to live that lasts beyond the grave.

"Sorry, I'm Working that Holiday"
by Debbie Miller

"Not that I speak in respect of want: for I have learned, in whatsoever state I am, therewith to be content." (Philippians 4:11)

As a cop's wife, you learn to live with burdens most wives don't have: concern for your spouse's safety, toxic media, and bad politics, just to name a few. I was also concerned about Brian bringing home "unwanted guests." I can't say how often I told him not to bring home roaches. Thankfully, he never did.

A more immediate, potentially frustrating day-to-day burden for a cop's wife is the work schedule. If your spouse works patrol, police work is 24/7/365, weekends and holidays. If he gets involved in some matter toward the end of the shift and goes into overtime, he has to do his job.

One Sunday, Brian was on day shift, scheduled to be off work at 2:30 pm. An assignment of an accident was broadcast at about 2:10. Brian took it. It turned out to be a fatal accident, which involved a detailed investigation. He didn't arrive home until after 10:30.

On 9/11, Brian was a boss in the downtown jail. He called me and said he could not leave. There was concern that heavily populated areas like downtown Cleveland would be easy targets for more attacks, so downtown was evacuated--except prisoners and police. Such is the life of a police officer and his family.

I knew of an officer's wife who struggled with her husband's work schedule and all the family gatherings he missed. She had not learned to be content about this matter which became a problem in their marriage.

Times may come when your husband can't attend important functions due to work. You may be at church, family gatherings, graduations, weddings, and other get-togethers alone. What do you do?

One thing you shouldn't do is complain and be discontented. You'll likely just cause friction with your spouse. Ever hear of the *"Proverbs 31"* woman? You may hear preachers talk about godly womanhood, and quote from *Proverbs 31*:

"Who can find a virtuous woman? For her price is far above rubies. The heart of her husband doth safely trust in her, so that he shall have no need of spoil. She will do him good and not evil all the days of her life." (Proverbs 31:10-12)

The chapter continues about her industrious nature, care for her family, kindness, and other virtues. But did you ever hear of the *"Proverbs 21"* woman? She's the evil twin of the *"Proverbs 31"* woman:

"It is better to dwell in a corner of the housetop, than

with a brawling woman in a wide house." (Proverbs 21:9) "It is better to dwell in the wilderness, than with a contentious and an angry woman." (Proverbs 21:19)

The *"Proverbs 21"* woman complains and argues. Don't be the *"Proverbs 21"* woman. If you make a habit of complaining, don't be surprised when your spouse vacates more to the garage, basement, or other *"corner of the housetop"*-type place to get away from you.

Paul said in our opening verse that he "learned" to be content, so apparently at some point he was not content with his circumstances. Yet God dealt with him and he learned to be content. If you're not content with your spouse's occupation, God can do the same with you as He did with Paul.

One way to make the best of your spouse's work schedule is to work around it. I am very organized and have kept a planning calendar for all my adult life. As a couple, we always lived and planned events by my calendar. If Brian worked Thanksgiving, we planned family dinner around his schedule. If he worked afternoons, dinner was about noon. If he worked days, dinner was closer to 5:00.

Christmas was always fun to fit into his schedule. If his regular days off were a day or so before the 25th, we would celebrate Christmas that day. If we celebrated Christmas on December 22 or 23, it worked for us. The kids didn't seem to know we were celebrating early. If they did, they still enjoyed it.

The Bible says *"In every thing give thanks: for this is the will of God in Christ Jesus concerning you." (1 Thessalonians 5:18)*

1. Thank the Lord for your spouse's job and willingness to work
2. Thank the Lord for holiday pay, which is usually extra.
3. Thank the Lord for your spouse's health and ability to work.

Your spouse's work schedule with all the functions he misses is hard for him too, not just you. Determine that by God's grace, you'll support your spouse and let the crazy work schedule bring you closer together, not farther apart.

Getting Back into the Game

"So when they had dined, Jesus saith to Simon Peter, Simon, son of Jonas, lovest thou me more than these? He saith unto him, Yea, Lord; thou knowest that I love thee. He saith unto him, Feed my lambs.

He saith to him again the second time, Simon, son of Jonas, lovest thou me? He saith unto him, Yea, Lord; thou knowest that I love thee. He saith unto him, Feed my sheep.

He saith unto him the third time, Simon, son of Jonas, lovest thou me? Peter was grieved because he said unto him the third time, Lovest thou me? And he said unto him, Lord, thou knowest all things; thou knowest that I love thee. Jesus saith unto him, Feed my sheep." (John 21:15-17)

Before Jesus was arrested, He warned His disciples that they would forsake Him. Peter didn't think *he'd* ever do that. When Jesus was arrested, though, Peter impulsively attacked a servant of the high priest and cut off his ear. He may have been aiming for his head, and the Lord let the swing be deflected and Jesus even healed the ear. Still, Peter had committed a serious crime.

Later, people told Peter that he'd been with Jesus. But Peter denied it. Three times. He may have lied only to avoid being arrested for assaulting the servant. Still, he denied the Lord, just as Jesus had said he'd do. He even cursed and swore. He may have used foul language.

110

Ever hear the phrase, "curse like a sailor"? Peter was a fisherman. Bad language may have been common among fishermen. It's certainly common among cops. Yet foul language is a lousy testimony for a Christian.

The Bible says he swore with an oath. Maybe he said, "I swear I don't know Him!" Like a guy you catch with drugs and he says, "Officer, I swear that's not my stuff!" or even, "I swear on my mother" or "I swear on my baby." Is that supposed to make them more believable? What are you supposed to say, "cross your heart, hope to die, stick a needle in your eye?"

Peter probably felt small later when he saw Jesus after He'd risen from the dead. Maybe Peter thought he'd messed up so badly that the Lord would never want to use him again. But the Lord forgave him and restored him. In fact, after Jesus ascended into heaven, Peter preached a mighty sermon at Pentecost and 3,000 souls were saved.

Peter wasn't the only Bible hero who had his bad moments. Noah once acted like a drunken slob. Abraham lied to protect himself—twice. Jacob masqueraded as his brother Esau to get his blessing from their father Isaac. David committed adultery with another man's wife.

Sin isn't ok because people in the Bible did it. In each case their sin brought bad results. Sin always does. But their stories show how gracious the Lord is to forgive and restore people and still use them for His glory.

In police work, it's easy to let your Christian life fall by the wayside. You work crazy hours. You see things most people never see, including most Christians. You deal all day long with profane, ungodly people (including cops), and you're tired after working part-time and overtime.

Maybe you're saved but you rarely go to church, and you can't remember the last time you read your Bible. Maybe your language and demeanor haven't been very Christlike. You know you should go to church, but you don't think it will do much good.

Well, look at how the Lord dealt with Peter. Peter's past failures probably haunted him, but the Lord didn't even mention them! When Jesus asked Peter if he loved Him and Peter said he did, Jesus didn't counter with, "Well, why did you deny me three times?"

No, the Lord told him to *"Feed my lambs"* and *"Feed my sheep."* Or to put it another way, "Let's get back to work. There are sinners who need to be reached and Christians who need to be helped."

Just as the Lord eagerly restored Peter to fellowship and service, He wants to do the same with you. That's why this story is in the Bible, to encourage you to get back into fellowship with the Lord, back into the game, back into the good fight of faith.

Easter Morning

"And we know that all things work together for good to them that love God, to them who are the called according to his purpose." (Romans 8:28)

One night before Easter, I was on a one-man car. I liked working alone. I could do what I wanted. If I wanted to back up a car on a gun run, make a traffic stop, or skip lunch, I didn't have to argue with a whiny partner. I worked with a guy who whined. He also had a whiny voice, which made his whining even worse.

About 2:36 a.m. one Easter morning, Dave Sumskis and Ricky Sheppard got a call to 10401 Eliot Avenue for a female holding a child hostage. I went to assist. I took East 104 north from Union Avenue and pretty much dead-ended right in front of the house. I arrived first. The street was dark and quiet. I saw two women in front of the house. I exited the car.

They said a mentally ill woman in the upstairs residence had a baby and had started a fire. As I walked up the front stairs one of them added, "And she might have a gun."

Great.

I walked through the front door into the downstairs residence, which was unoccupied. I noticed a nasty chemical smell. I walked through the house, then up the back steps to the upstairs residence.

I opened the door into the kitchen. Right in front of me, something was smoking on the stove. At the far corner to my right, in the doorway to the living room, stood a small woman: 40ish, button-down off-white shirt, black stirrup pants. I saw something was wrong with her just by looking at her. I also saw something in her right hand, but her arm swung behind the wall before I caught what it was.

"Don't follow me," she said quietly. Nothing else. She turned and disappeared into the living room.

I walked to the doorway where she'd been. I looked into the living room, gun drawn. No one there. The living room was dark. I saw a set of French doors across the room. I walked over to them, opened one, and walked in.

It was a bedroom. To my left, the woman stood in an entryway of a hall that led back to the kitchen. In front of me was a bed. On the bed lay a small baby, maybe a few months old. Now I saw what was in the woman's hand: a gun. It was pointed toward the floor. "Don't take the baby," she said quietly. Nothing else.

I turned to her, gun pointed. "Sweetheart, drop the gun," I said. I don't usually use flirty phrases like that, but that's what occurred to me at the time.

Unfortunately, Sweetheart didn't drop the gun. I'm not sure she even understood me. I had a flashlight in my right hand. I tucked it under my left, hoping to grab the baby with my right.

Meanwhile, Dave and Ricky had come in the same way I had. I didn't see them, but she'd heard the noise they made and become agitated. She started looking back and forth: toward them, then back to me, back and forth, like she wasn't sure what to do.

Then she turned to me. The gun started to come up. About the time it was aimed at my thighs, I fired twice. Both shots missed.

She ran down the hall toward Dave and Ricky. She stopped at the entry to the kitchen and took a shooting stance. I saw her in profile and knew she was aiming at someone. I took a position along one of the French doors and fired four rounds. She jerked up, wobbled around, then fell into the bathroom across from the kitchen. The baby on the bed started screaming from the gunfire.

I went down the hall to the kitchen. Ricky was on the floor. She'd grazed his jacket with a bullet. "She's still got the gun!" He yelled. I looked over. She lay on her side on the floor, gun in hand. She was trying to raise it, but she was weak.

I stepped over to her, took the gun from her hand, and

put it on top of a refrigerator. Dave had come up behind Ricky. "Get the baby out!" he ordered. Someone—I don't know who—got the baby out of the apartment.

I reloaded my gun and went to the bathroom to check on the woman on the floor. If she moved at all, it wasn't much. I saw a pool of blood under her stomach. I don't know how I thought to say this, but I bent down and said to her, "If you ask Jesus to save you, He will."

I left the apartment. Sgt. Jim Oryl was also on scene, as well as Officers Matt Ewing and John Traine. The paramedics came down with the gurney carrying the woman. Matt was nearby.

"How is she?" I asked.

Matt shook his head. "She's dead."

One of the women I'd seen at the start of this incident came by.

"What happened?" she asked.

"I shot her," I replied curtly. I shouldn't have said it like that, but I was in a really crummy mood.

"WHAT DO YOU MEAN, YOU SHOT HER?" She cried.

"YOU SAID YOU NEEDED HELP!" I snapped

angrily. Like I said, I was in a really crummy mood.

Sgt. Oryl stood nearby. "Get him out of here!" he ordered John. John collared me and took me to the patrol car. We sat and waited for personnel from Homicide, Internal Affairs, and the Crime Scene Unit—collectively known as "the shooting team"—to show up.

As we sat and waited in the dark, John encouraged me. "You've been through this before," he offered. I had. This was my second shooting, but the first where I shot the suspect. Having him and Matt there helped.

The shooting team showed up and investigated. Ricky had to go to the hospital so we could be sure he didn't have any holes in him that we didn't know about. He told me later that she appeared out of nowhere with a gun pointed at him. When she fired at him, he spun and fired back. When I'd seen her in a shooting stance, she was firing at Ricky.

About 9:00 am, we were finally cleared to leave. I went home, cleaned up, and went to church. I was too keyed up to sleep. That night I sang in the church choir for our Easter special. Talk about going from one extreme to the other.

The shooting was in the morning paper the day after Easter. The story included how my first two shots had missed, which happened because the flashlight under

117

my left arm had thrown off my aim. Monday morning, I went to Homicide to meet investigators and return to the scene for a walk-through.

Dennis Gunsch was a sergeant in Internal Affairs. He and I were headed out the door of headquarters to go to the scene. As we were walking out, Joe Paskvan was walking in. Joe had about seventeen years on the job. He had also been a Marine in Vietnam. Tough as nails, but a heart of gold. I was still in a crummy mood. "Hi, Joe," I mumbled, barely looking at him.

He didn't say "hi" back. He must have read the paper. "WHAT DO YOU MEAN, THE FIRST TWO SHOTS MISSED?" he chided. "WHAT KIND OF MARINE ARE YOU?" Then he burst out laughing. "If you need anything, let me know," he said as he walked away smiling. Dennis shook his head in disbelief.

Joe's crazy humor actually helped cheer me up. For Joe to yank my chain like that, especially after all he'd been through in Vietnam and several police shootings, I knew that he was concerned and sincere.

I was off the street for about one-and-a-half months with the investigation. After the prosecutor cleared me, I went back to patrol at the 4th District.

About two weeks after my return, we had a call of a mental male in a house alone. Long story short, I made the not-so-smart decision to break into the house and go after him. We fought. I lost my balance. He actually stood over me at one point with a garden hoe raised over me, but for some miraculous reason, he didn't swing it. Eventually we took him into custody.

Back at the station a little later my boss, Sgt. Sharon Lorenc, spoke with me. She very quietly said, "Brian, there was no baby in the house, and no need to go in like that." She didn't give me a public whipping, although I probably deserved it for being reckless. She obviously could tell that the Easter morning shooting was still heavy on my mind.

As for our Scripture, how could something as bad as this work out for good? Well, any or all of us could have been killed. This could have been a murder-suicide. She'd started a fire and was walking around with a gun. She'd even told me not to take the baby, which told me that she had some sinister intentions for the baby.

I was also proud of Dave and Ricky. Dave had also been a Vietnam Marine--Force Recon—and even after Vietnam and 17 years on the job, he was still gung-ho. Ricky was young, but definitely on his "A" game.

I'm especially grateful to the Lord for grace to go from cop-in-a-shooting mode to tell-someone-about-Jesus mode. I don't know if she'd heard what I'd said. I don't know that she hadn't. It may have been her last chance to accept Christ, like the thief on the cross.

I also had the experience—not that I wanted it—of killing a suspect. No decent officer wants to do that, but when a suspect presents a deadly threat and the officer has no other reasonable choice, the fault is the suspect's, not the officer's. Having been there, though, I've been able to identify with and minister to other cops who would later go through the same thing.

Use of deadly force also has an emotional angle as well as a legal angle. During the incident itself, you're just acting on instinct, shooting to save life. Personally, I felt crummy for a while after the incident: not "guilty" crummy, but more like "Why did this have to happen?" crummy. But that feeling passed as time went on.

I'd also never met an officer who was happy about having killed a suspect. Many had peace of mind that they'd done the right thing, which they should have, but they weren't rejoicing at the loss of life.

One final note: around 1998, I pulled over a young lady on a traffic stop. She had no ID, but she needed to identify herself. She pulled an envelope out of the glove box with her name and address. She handed it to me. My eyes widened at the address: 10401 Eliot.

"Wasn't there an incident some years back with some woman and the police there?" I kept my question purposely vague.

"Yeah, there was. Some woman got into it with the

police," she replied.

"Wasn't there some baby involved, too?"

"Yeah."

"What was the baby's name?"

"Samona."

"How is the baby doing now?"

"She's fine."

She never seemed curious why I was asking.

Graham v. Connor

"The grass withereth, the flower fadeth: but the word of our God shall stand for ever. " (Isaiah 40:8)

Need proof that there is a God? *Psalm 19:1* says, *"The heavens declare the glory of God; and the firmament sheweth his handiwork."* At the right time of year, you'll see the constellations Orion and Pleiades. Also, when you see the Big Dipper, follow its handle from the bowl outward. The bright star a little distance away is Arcturus.

All three of these are mentioned in *Job 9:9*: *"[God] Which maketh Arcturus, Orion, and Pleiades, and the chambers of the south."*

God also gave us the Bible to tell us what we need to know about Him. God inspired the writers of the Bible over hundreds of years: from Moses, who wrote Genesis, to the Apostle John, who wrote Revelation. God inspired them to write words that would never become outdated or obsolete. That's why the verse says, *"...the word of our God shall stand for ever."*

As a cop, you have written standards to go by: law books, rules of evidence, and policies. You need written standards to know what you can and can't do. If you abide by them, they also protect you if your actions are called into question in a trial or lawsuit.

You've probably gone to a break-in and the victim has told you, "They robbed my house!" You know that houses aren't robbed, they're burglarized. But don't tell your victim that. He's already in a lousy mood. He doesn't need you being a smart aleck. Just write it up as a burglary.

You also know about *Graham v. Connor*, the Supreme Court decision for police use of force. *Graham* says any force you use must be objectively reasonable based on circumstances. Before *Graham,* states had individual use-of-force standards, but after *Graham,* all other standards are outdated and obsolete. Nothing new, however, will ever come along to make the Bible outdated or obsolete.

God knows all there is to know. Even things we don't yet know, God knows already: *"...his understanding is infinite." (Psalm 147:5)* New inventions and tech advances are great. *Daniel 12:4* says that in later times, life will be fast-paced and people will know more: *"...many shall run to and fro, and knowledge shall be increased."* We see the truth of this prophecy with cars, planes, computers, cell phones, and the internet.

No new discovery will ever be made, however, to make the Bible obsolete: *"Thy word is true from the beginning: and every one of thy righteous judgments endureth for ever." (Psalm 119:160)* People still try to discredit God's Word, though, so certain verses are in His Word for spiritual "firewalls" from false beliefs.

123

Evolution has never been proven, and the truth of *Genesis 1:1, "In the beginning God created the heaven and the earth.",* still stands.

People may believe in and fear man-made climate change, and governments may spend taxpayer money supposedly to fight it, but *Genesis 8:22* assures us it won't destroy the earth. *"While the earth remaineth, seedtime and harvest, and COLD AND HEAT* [capitals mine]*, and summer and winter, and day and night shall not cease."*

God's Word also won't change with culture. With God, there is no such thing as same-sex marriage or gender identity: *"...he which made them at the beginning* [they didn't evolve, God made them; Jesus said so] *made them male and female," (Matthew 19:4)* Same-gender people may be physically intimate and enter into what they call marriage, but it's not marriage to God.

People are also the gender that God made them, no matter how they feel, dress, or act. Inclinations to these behaviors are just temptations from the devil.

Most of all, Jesus said in *Matthew 24:35, "Heaven and earth shall pass away, but my words shall not pass away."* The good news of Jesus' death for our sins, and His burial and resurrection, will always be a message from God to touch hearts, save souls, and change lives.

Aim to Please

"And whatsoever we ask, we receive of him, because we keep his commandments, and do those things that are pleasing in his sight." (1 John 3:22)

When you receive the Lord Jesus as your Saviour, something wonderful happens: you become a child of God: *"For ye are all the children of God by faith in Christ Jesus." (Galatians 3:26)* You also become a servant of God: *"But now being made free from sin, and become servants to God, ye have your fruit unto holiness, and the end everlasting life." (Romans 6:22)*

As God's servant, you have the most important purpose in the world to live, too: to serve and please the Lord who saved you: *"...as ye have received of us how ye ought to walk and to please God, so ye would abound more and more." (1 Thessalonians 4:1)*

The happiest way to live your Christian life, as our verse says, is to strive to obey God (*"...we keep his commandments,"*) and to please Him in your daily life (*"...and do those things that are pleasing in his sight."*)

Unfortunately, even in a good church you may find people who don't do these. They may not attend church faithfully, only read their Bible or pray once in a while, and make little or no effort to reach lost people. As a result, their Christian life is not joyful or productive.

Cops can be that way about the job. As a cop, you need to resist the temptation to stagnate. Cops may say things like, "The city doesn't want you to work", which may be partly true, but cops may say things like that to excuse their laziness. No matter what "the city" or anyone else says, citizens need you to do your best.

Think of police work, not as a service to "the city", but as a service to the Lord, which it is, anyway. When you focus on pleasing the Lord with your best work, catching bad guys and helping decent people, you'll find that you enjoy the job more, even after many years and even despite all the opposition cops get nowadays.

At times you may not feel like working, but you do anyway, right? It's much the same with your Christian life. At times you may not want to go to church, read your Bible, pray, or serve. Do these anyway, because God said to, no matter how you feel. Obedience pleases God, and you'll see that God blesses obedience.

As for pleasing God, this next point is a little lengthy but it's important. *1 Corinthians 7:32-34* says in part, *"...He that is unmarried careth...how he may please the Lord: But he that is married careth for...how he may please his wife."* and *"...The unmarried woman careth for the things of the Lord...but she that is married careth for...how she may please her husband."*

This passage speaks primarily of the contrast between married Christians and unmarried. Singles don't have a spouse to care about and can concentrate more on serving the Lord. Married Christians, however, need to think about pleasing their spouses, as well.

It doesn't mean Christians shouldn't marry, but it contains a simple piece of advice: *If you want a happy marriage, do things to please your spouse.*

The passage talks of the man, *"...how he may **please** his wife."* and of the wife, *"...how she may **please** her husband."* (boldfaces added)

When you were dating the person who's now your spouse, you probably did things to please him/her: bought flowers or gifts, sent cards, left notes, talked on the phone.

These all took effort and/or expense, but they pleased your loved one and you enjoyed the relationship more. If you still do these things after you're married, they'll help your marriage. If you've stopped doing these things, start up again. Do things to please your spouse.

Likewise, do things to please your Saviour. Obey Him even if you don't feel like it. Thank Him often for saving you. Spend time in His Word and think on it often. Ask Him to use it to speak to your heart and ask Him to help you tell others about Him. Doing these will help you live a Christian life that pleases Him and is happier for you.

A Relationship, not a Job

"Now it came to pass, as they went, that he entered into a certain village: and a certain woman named Martha received him into her house. And she had a sister called Mary, which also sat at Jesus' feet, and heard his word. But Martha was cumbered about much serving, and came to him, and said, Lord, dost thou not care that my sister hath left me to serve alone? bid her therefore that she help me. And Jesus answered and said unto her, Martha, Martha, thou art careful and troubled about many things: But one thing is needful: and Mary hath chosen that good part, which shall not be taken away from her." (Luke 10:38-42)

One day Jesus visited Mary and Martha. Martha worked hard to make a meal for the Lord to enjoy, and she was probably a great cook, but she became *"cumbered about much serving."* Apparently, she was so focused on making sure everything was perfect that she was missing the main point of Jesus' visit: fellowship with Jesus Himself.

Martha saw Mary was just sitting there, not helping, and wanted the Lord to tell Mary to help. Martha was apparently so stressed out that she was even a little accusing toward the Lord: *"...Lord, dost thou not care...?"* What a thing to say! Of course He cared!

No doubt Martha meant well, but she had too much on her plate. She was, as Jesus said, *"careful and troubled about many things."* The one thing that was needful, as the Lord said, was spending time in fellowship with Jesus.

That's what Mary was doing. She wasn't just sitting around doing nothing. She *"...sat at Jesus' feet, and heard his word."* When she was at Jesus' feet, she could hear what He had to say and respond to it.

Imagine visiting a friend. He's glad to see you but gets so busy preparing food that he's not spending time with you. Even if he means well, he's defeating the purpose of the visit. That's how Martha was. The Lord wasn't there for the food. He was there for her and Mary.

Marriage can be that way. God intended for marriage to be a relationship, not a job. But marriage takes work, especially with kids. He works. Sometimes he works part-time (one thing nice about police work is being able to work part-time). Sometimes she works. Both of them take care of kids: feeding, clothing, playing, schoolwork.

With all the work of child-rearing and running a household, and even with good intentions, a man and woman can miss fellowship with each other. That's why husbands and wives need to spend time together, strengthening their relationship, when they can.

The Christian life is also a relationship between Jesus

and the believer, not a job. Yes, the Bible talks about service, especially soul winning. Jesus Himself said,

"The harvest truly is plenteous, but the labourers are few; Pray ye therefore the Lord of the harvest, that he will send forth labourers into his harvest." (Matthew 9:37-38)

Service, however, is another area of fellowship with the Lord: *"For we are labourers together with God:" (1 Corinthians 3:9)* Not "for" God, but "with" God. Martha meant well, but she was so busy serving that she was missing out on fellowship with Jesus.

We don't see Jesus today as Martha and Mary did, but we can still have joy "sitting at Jesus' feet" by reading His Word, and by talking with Him in praise, prayer, and confession. That is the needful "good part" that Mary had.

As a believer in Christ, you have so many ways you can serve the Lord and reach people with the gospel. But please don't let personal Bible and prayer time get lost in the shuffle. Don't miss *"...that good part..."* that Mary had when she *"...sat at Jesus' feet, and heard his word."*

You Don't Really Want That

"...As I live, saith the Lord GOD, I have no pleasure in the death of the wicked; but that the wicked turn from his way and live:" (Ezekiel 33:11)

Say you get a call of a robbery at gunpoint. You fly to the scene. You pull up and see the suspect drive off. You follow. He takes off. He runs red lights and stop signs. He almost hits innocent people. He doesn't care. You pursue. You watch for traffic and pedestrians because, unlike him, you care about people.

That's a big difference between cops and criminals. Cops risk their lives to benefit others. Criminals risk others' lives to benefit themselves. During the chase, you fight to stay calm as you pursue and broadcast (and pray). Finally, your suspect loses control of the car and smashes into a pole.

You pull up, exit the patrol car, and run toward the suspect's car. He's pinned inside. You see flames under the mangled hood and gasoline all over the pavement. Your suspect is screaming. What do you do? Smile as the flame makes its way to the gasoline and the car explodes? After your suspect pointed a gun at the store clerk, then almost got you and a lot of innocent citizens killed, shame on him, right?

Wrong. You'd try your best to save him. First be sure that he can't get to a weapon. After all, he is still a violent criminal. Once you've done that, though, you'd even risk your own life to save him. Does he deserve your help? No, but that's beside the point. It's not about what he deserves. It's about how you value human life, and he needs your help, regardless of how he got into his predicament to begin with.

Now if the car blew up and he died, you wouldn't be glad. You'd have *"...no pleasure in the death of the wicked;"* even if his death were his fault--which it would have been. It'd be a gruesome memory.

Each of us, in a way, is like the robber. Maybe we've not committed violent crime, but we've all sinned against God: *"For all have sinned, and come short of the glory of God;" (Romans 3:23)* Like the robber, also, we've put ourselves in danger of death: not just physical death, but eternal death in hell: *"For the wages of sin is death;" "And death and hell were cast into the lake of fire." (Romans 6:23, Revelation 20:14)*

Yet the Lord Jesus hung on the cross, with the pain and mockery, and said, *"Father, forgive them; for they know not what they do." (Luke 23:34)* None of us deserved to have the Lord put His life on the line to save us, but it's not about what we deserve. It's about the Lord's love for us and willingness to save us, despite the fact that we'd put ourselves into trouble to begin with.

As a cop, you'll meet people who don't act right, live

right, dress right, or talk right. No doubt people act as they do because they don't know the true God, the God of the Bible. They may know some things *about* Him, but they don't *know* Him because they've not received the Lord Jesus as their personal Saviour. *1 Corinthians 15:34* says,*"...some have not the knowledge of God:"*

Yet God doesn't want to see those people die in their sins. There's no celebration in heaven when a sinner dies lost. There is, however, a big celebration in heaven when a sinner repents and accepts Jesus: *"...there is joy in the presence of the angels of God over one sinner that repenteth." (Luke 15:10)*

This is What Friends Do

"Now when Job's three friends heard of all this evil that was come upon him, they came...to mourn with him and to comfort him. So they sat down with him upon the ground seven days and seven nights, and none spake a word unto him: for they saw that his grief was very great." (Job 2:11, 13)

Job was very wealthy, but he feared and served God. God even said to Satan, *"Hast thou considered my servant Job, that there is none like him in the earth, a perfect and an upright man, one that feareth God, and escheweth evil?" (Job 1:8)*

Satan said Job only served God because God blessed him, and if God let Job suffer loss, Job would curse God to His face. God knew that wasn't true. He knew Job's heart, since God *"...knowest the hearts of all men," (Acts 1:24)* Still, God let Satan bring adversity into Job's life.

Here are some lessons in this passage: first, if you strive to honor the Lord, He is pleased: *"...such as are upright in their way are his delight." (Proverbs 11:20)*

Second, if you're saved and you strive to honor God, you'll likely face more temptation than a lazy Christian who doesn't serve the Lord. Third, Satan can only do what God lets him. Fourth, for some reason God may let Satan bring bad things into the lives of people who please Him.

Back to the story: Once Satan stepped in, Job's animals were stolen and destroyed, his servants were murdered, his seven sons died in a house collapse, and he was covered with boils from head to foot. His friends came *"...to mourn with him and to comfort him."* They even *"...sat down with him upon the ground seven days and seven nights,"* They must have been close friends to take that much time out of their lives.

One thing you can do if you want to share the gospel is to *"...weep with them that weep." (Romans 12:15)* When you know someone is having a bad time, reach out. If someone has lost a loved one, send a card, even if you don't know him or her. If you don't know what to say, keep it simple: "I'm sorry about the death of your (fill in the blank)."

If you ever lost a loved one, what did people say? Probably things like "I'm sorry", or "If you need anything, call me" or "I'm praying for you." You've probably said similar things to others who've lost loved ones. The words don't matter so much as the fact that people show concern.

The scripture also says of Job's friends, *"...and none spake a word unto him: for they saw that his grief was very great."* What would you say to someone who's lost seven kids? They may not have known what to say, but the fact that they were there no doubt meant a lot.

If someone is going through a tough situation that you have not been through, you can still be helpful and encouraging. Even if you don't know what to say, your physical presence or even a card can help.

Maybe you know of an officer who was in a shooting or other serious event. If you haven't been in a shooting—many officers have not--you may feel unsure if you should reach out.

Well, you should! Send a card, text, or email. Even if it's simple, send something! I was in several shootings and received emails, text messages, and phone calls letting me know people cared. It didn't matter to me how much experience any of them had on the job. It mattered that they were kind enough to reach out.

After a shooting, especially, you're taken away from people you work with. You're off the street. Your name and photo may be on the news. Your actions are investigated. You're questioned. You're even given your Miranda rights. All this investigation is necessary but it's no fun. If you're in a situation like that, wouldn't you want to hear from people close to you?

If you're not sure what to say, keep it simple: "I'm glad you're ok"; "You did a great job" "If you need anything, call me." If you don't know the officer, introduce yourself: "I'm John Doe from the 3rd District. I'm glad you're ok." Even if the officer doesn't reply, he'll appreciate the gesture.

Skeletons in Your Closet

"And the scribes and Pharisees brought unto him a woman taken in adultery; and when they had set her in the midst, They say unto him, Master, this woman was taken in adultery, in the very act. Now Moses in the law commanded us, that such should be stoned: but what sayest thou? This they said, tempting him, that they might have to accuse him. But Jesus stooped down, and with his finger wrote on the ground, as though he heard them not. So when they continued asking him, he lifted up himself, and said unto them, He that is without sin among you, let him first cast a stone at her. And again he stooped down, and wrote on the ground. And they which heard it, being convicted by their own conscience, went out one by one, beginning at the eldest, even unto the last: and Jesus was left alone, and the woman standing in the midst. When Jesus had lifted up himself, and saw none but the woman, he said unto her, Woman, where are those thine accusers? Hath no man condemned thee? She said, No man, Lord. And Jesus said unto her, Neither do I condemn thee: go and sin no more." (John 8:3-11)

The scribes and Pharisees brought a woman taken in adultery, *"in the very act"*. That's interesting. How do you find a woman *"in the very act"* of adultery unless you know where to look? They obviously knew.

If they went to a brothel and grabbed a prostitute, it means they knew where the brothel was. Also interesting. And where was the man? Wasn't he committing adultery, too? Doesn't it take two to commit adultery?

Truth is, they weren't trying to condemn her. They were trying to condemn Jesus. They'd hoped He'd contradict Moses. The Lord knew the game they were playing. He ignored them and wrote on the ground. Then He said, *"He that is without sin among you, let him first cast a stone at her."* Then He continued to write on the ground.

No one knows what He wrote. The Bible doesn't say. Maybe He was writing down their sins. After all, He was God in the flesh, and the Lord *"...knoweth the secrets of the heart." (Psalm 44:21)* Jesus knew their dirty little secrets, too. Maybe He had started a list with the sins of the oldest Pharisees, then on down to the younger, which is why the older ones left first.

At any rate, they left one by one. Interestingly, they didn't leave out of fear of public embarrassment or exposure. They left because their consciences bothered them. God was dealing with their hearts.

Eventually Jesus was alone with the woman. Yes, she was guilty, but her accusers were gone. Jesus could have accused her, but that's not why He came to earth. *John 3:17* says, *"For God sent not his Son into the world to condemn the world; but that the world through him might be saved."* She recognized Him as Lord, trusted in Him as Saviour, and she was free from condemnation for her sin.

It's wonderful to have Jesus as Saviour. The Lord knows all about us, even our sins that no one else knows about. When you receive Jesus as Saviour, your whole sin-debt of past, present, and future is forgiven: *"As far as the east is from the west, so far hath he removed our transgressions from us." (Psalm 103:12)*

The scribes and Pharisees obviously didn't care one bit about this woman. She was just a pawn in some deceitful game they were trying to play. Yet God even used their treachery to bring her face to face with the One who would give her the forgiveness and salvation she needed.

Use the Brains God Gave You

"Thy word is true from the beginning:"
(Psalm 119:160)

In February 2014, Ken Ham debated Bill Nye "the Science Guy" about earth's origin. Ham is a Bible believer and creationist; Nye, an evolutionist (info taken from *youngearth.org*). Both men presented evidences, but neither position can be proven scientifically, because earth's origin cannot be re-created. Facts can be interpreted differently. Some believe, for example, that the Grand Canyon was formed by evolution. Others believe it was formed by a worldwide flood.

Believing the Bible, though, is not unscientific or ignorant. God's Word never condemns any search for knowledge, which is what science is about. Luke the gospel author was a doctor--*"Luke, the beloved physician, and Demas, greet you." (Colossians 4:14)*-- so apparently he studied medicine and the sciences associated with it, like biology and chemistry.

Jesus Himself spoke of doctors: *"They that be whole need not a physician, but they that are sick." (Matthew 9:12)* The prophet Daniel was educated in science, too. When King Nebuchadnezzar picked certain Jews to train in the ways of Babylon, he wanted people who were *"...skillful in all wisdom, and cunning in knowledge, and understanding science," (Daniel 1:4).*

The apostle Paul also warned Timothy to avoid *"...oppositions of science falsely so called:" (1 Timothy 6:20) "Science falsely so called"* is something that's called science but isn't. Evolution is not science. Biology, physics, and chemistry are all sciences. They can be proven. Evolution can't be proven.

Still, many people may believe in evolution because it's the only "scientific" explanation for earth's origin that they've heard. Moreover, if they go to church at all, they may go to a place where the Bible is not respected as God's Word, so they've learned to think that evolution is science and Bible stories are just religious fairy tales.

It's also probably fair to say that most people don't have an advanced scientific education like Ham or Nye, so they can't argue science on a sophisticated level.

Yet God's Word has an answer. Jesus said we were created: *"But from the beginning of the creation God made them male and female." (Mark 10:6)*

He also said that the flood--and the fiery overthrow of Sodom and Gomorrha—really happened:

"And as it was in the days of Noe, so shall it be also in the days of the Son of man. They did eat, they drank, they married wives, they were given in marriage, until the day that Noe entered into the ark, and the flood came, and destroyed them all. Likewise also as it was

141

in the days of Lot; they did eat, they drank, they bought, they sold, they planted, they builded; But the same day that Lot went out of Sodom it rained fire and brimstone from heaven, and destroyed them all." (Luke 17:26-29)

Jesus also said the time before His Second Coming would be like the days of Noah and Lot, marked by violence, religious deception, and rampant sin: *"And then shall many be offended, and shall betray one another, and shall hate one another. And many false prophets shall rise, and shall deceive many. And because iniquity shall abound, the love of many shall wax cold."* (Matthew 24:10-12) Cops especially see the violence and sin up close, more than most people.

Now if Jesus said these things happened and they hadn't, then He was just a phony and a liar, His death on the cross meant nothing, and He wouldn't have risen again. Yet over five hundred people saw Him after He'd risen: *"...he was seen of above five hundred brethren at once;"* (1 Corinthians 15:6)

By His resurrection, He demonstrated that He's God the Son, worthy of worship, and the Saviour of all who will believe on Him; and that His words are true and trustworthy, including His words about creation.

Destroyed for Lack of Knowledge

"My people are destroyed for lack of knowledge: because thou hast rejected knowledge, I will also reject thee, that thou shalt be no priest to me:" (Hosea 4:6)

The Heimlich maneuver, without a doubt, has saved many people from choking to death. What if you were at a picnic, though, and someone started choking and no one did the Heimlich? The victim would grab his throat and he'd turn an ugly color. He'd fall down and likely pass out. Someone may call 911, but if he died before help arrived, it could be said that he was destroyed for lack of knowledge, because no one came forward who knew the Heimlich maneuver.

Our verse also talks about people being destroyed for lack of knowledge. It says that they're destroyed for lack of knowledge of the true God. God gave us the Bible to give us knowledge about Him: how to worship, serve, and fellowship with Him.

One important reason for church is for people to hear God's Word preached and how to apply it to their personal lives. Yet if a so-called "minister" won't preach God's Word to his congregation, they risk being *"destroyed for lack of knowledge."*

Hosea the prophet had written this book at a time when Israel didn't want to obey God or hear His Word. They wanted to enjoy their sin like the heathen around

143

them. They went through religious motions, but their lives were consistent with *Mark 7:6: "...This people honoureth me with their lips, but their heart is far from me."*

As a cop, you see how sin enslaves and destroys people's lives. People need to hear God's Word. People need to hear how to repent and turn to Christ to be saved. Once they've received Christ, they need strong Bible preaching and teaching to grow as Christians.

For all these reasons, believers in Christ need to share God's Word with others: to tell people how to receive Jesus as Saviour and how to live for Him. God's Word is called *"the sword of the Spirit," (Ephesians 6:17).* It's *"...quick, and powerful, and sharper than any two-edged sword," (Hebrews 4:12)*

God uses it to perform miracles in people's hearts and lives. That's why those who know Jesus as Saviour need to share God's Word with others, so they won't be eternally *"destroyed for lack of knowledge."*

Back to the picnic: say the ambulance is driving away with the choking victim. People are standing around in shock, worried, and crying. What would you think if one of the people there said, "I know the Heimlich maneuver, but I wasn't sure I should use it"?

One night several of our vice officers were involved in a shooting. They were ok. The young suspect wasn't.

I learned later that he'd been armed and chasing another young man. The cops happened to be nearby. They exited their vehicle and ordered him to stop. He turned and fired on them. They returned fire and hit him.

I went to the suspect. The cops were a distance away. I leaned over him as he lay on the street. "Turn me over on my back," he asked quietly. He was already on his back. That should have clued me in that he was in bad shape.

I'd love to say at this point that I told him how to receive Jesus as his Saviour and he did, but I'd be lying. I had the time to say something to him about Christ, but to my shame, I said nothing. Did I not think he was hurt that badly? Was I afraid to offend the cops he'd just shot at? It doesn't matter. I should have said something but didn't.

After a minute or so, his eyes started to roll back into his head. I knew then that he was headed into eternity, but the paramedic walked up and started working on him. I may have mumbled a quick prayer for the Lord to reach him, but my chance to witness was gone. Forever. He died.

If you're saved, you know something far more important than the Heimlich maneuver. You know how people can be forgiven and saved for eternity. Ask the Lord to guide and help you to share Christ with people, so they won't be *destroyed for lack of knowledge.*

Cleaning House

"And Jesus went into the temple of God, and cast out all them that sold and bought in the temple, and overthrew the tables of the moneychangers, and the seats of them that sold doves, And said unto them, It is written, My house shall be called the house of prayer; but ye have made it a den of thieves."
(Matthew 21:12-13)

The temple was supposed to be a special place to worship God and pray, but people had turned it into a dishonest money-making racket. The Lord went into the temple and literally cleaned house! It must have been a sight: Jesus overturning tables and ordering the moneychangers out. They'd defiled God's house like that, so they deserved the treatment Jesus gave them.

When Jesus entered the temple, He cleaned out the sin that was going on inside. One lesson from this story is that when Jesus comes into the temple, He cleans out sin. Our story also applies to another temple where the Lord wants to "clean house": the human temple.

When a person receives the Lord Jesus as Saviour, the Lord takes up residence inside. *Colossians 1:27* talks about *"...Christ in you, the hope of glory:"* *1 John 4:4* also says, *"...greater is he that is in you, than he that is in the world."* *1 Corinthians 3:16* asks believers in Christ, *"Know ye not that ye are the temple of God, and that the Spirit of God dwelleth in you?"*

146

How does Jesus come in? Only one way: consent. Jesus waits for consent. As a cop, you know you can only enter a place by consent, a warrant, or an exigent circumstance (basically a life-threatening emergency). Jesus doesn't force Himself into a person's life, however. He only comes into a person's life as Saviour by their consent.

Ever ask to go into someone's house and he asked, "Do you have a warrant?" If he didn't let you in, he may just not like the police in his house. Or he may have had something to hide. If you enter a house and find something illegal or fruits of a crime, you may arrest the owner or occupant if you entered and obtained these items legally. Once you're inside, you can deal officially with whatever you find that's illegal.

Someone may give you consent because he has nothing to hide. Or he may have something to hide but doesn't realize it. A guy on one traffic stop told me, "You can check me. You can check my car."

That sounded like consent to me, so I checked his car. I saw a rolled-up piece of brown, sandwich bag-type paper sticking out of his cigarette lighter. I pulled it out and unrolled it. Inside were several rocks of crack cocaine. He said I could check his car, didn't he?

When you receive Jesus as Saviour, you're giving Him consent to "deal officially" with you about things you should and shouldn't do. It's not always comfortable, but it's always right. As He cleaned out the temple, He wants to clean you—His human temple—to help you please Him and serve Him better.

An important part of being a Christian is reading God's Word and hearing Bible sermons preached. God speaks to our hearts about changes we need to make. It's great when the Lord works in your life to bring changes, and He blesses as you honor and obey Him.

Thinking Outside the Badge

"Likewise, ye wives, be in subjection to your own husbands; that, if any obey not the word, they also may without the word be won by the conversation of the wives;" (1 Peter 3:1)

You've heard of "going outside the box," doing something in a little unusual way. Our verse talks a little about going "outside the box" in order to win people to Christ. It tells how a woman who knows Jesus as Saviour should act toward her unsaved husband.

The Bible says saved people should not marry unsaved people: *"Be ye not unequally yoked together with unbelievers:" (2 Corinthians 6:14)* But what if neither spouse is saved, but the wife hears the gospel and accepts Christ, but her husband is still unsaved? Now what?

Our verse says wives should *"be in subjection to your own husbands;"* She should strive to love and respect him, whether he's saved or not. Maybe she's tried to talk with him about Jesus and he's not been receptive, but she can still pray for him, strive to live right, and be a good wife. Even if he won't *"obey the word,"*—he doesn't want to hear about "her religion", God uses her conduct (her "conversation") to convince him "outside the box", *"...without the word...",* to receive Jesus as Saviour.

The same principle applies to a husband with an unsaved wife. He should still treat her with love, respect, and affection, yet still pray for her and strive to live right. She'll see the changes that Jesus makes in his life, she'll know why he acts as he does, and God uses his "conversation" to deal with her heart *"...without the word..."* about accepting Jesus as Saviour, too.

As a cop, you need to think outside the box sometimes. It's not just about enforcing law, but also about dealing with people. Most people who break the law know they messed up, but how you deal with them is important. You've probably heard people say things like, "The police arrested me, but they treated me ok," or on the flip side, "Ok, I deserved a ticket, but the cop was such a jerk."

Say you're at a domestic. The man has an old traffic warrant. He's not a bad guy, but he has to go to jail and his small kids are nearby. Don't cuff him in front of his kids, so they can cry because daddy's going to jail and "everybody knows what police do to people in jail."

Get the kids away if you can. If they see what's going on, put him into the car, then come back and reassure them that daddy will be okay. You might say daddy had to take care of something and he'll be out of jail soon (depending on how long mommy takes to raise the bail money). Doing things out of common decency is a good way to enhance people's ideas about the police while still doing your job.

Thinking outside the box will help you reach people on the job for Christ, too. Don't whine, gossip, or badmouth people, even if you think they deserve it. Ask the Lord to help you serve Him on the job with a right heart. *"...out of the abundance of the heart the mouth speaketh." (Matthew 12:34)*

Strive to be helpful and do more than your share of the work (unlike those who like to do less than their share of the work). If people know that you're saved and your "walk" matches your "talk", God can use your "conversation" to touch people's hearts *"...without the word..."* and open a door to talk about Christ.

Trick Questions

"Then certain of the scribes and of the Pharisees answered, saying, Master, we would see a sign from thee. But he [Jesus] answered and said unto them, An evil and adulterous generation seeketh after a sign; and there shall no sign be given to it, but the sign of the prophet Jonas: For as Jonas was three days and three nights in the whale's belly; so shall the Son of man be three days and three nights in the heart of the earth."
(Matthew 12:38-40)

Why did these people ask Jesus for a sign? Were they honestly seeking proof that He was the Messiah? Or did they have an ulterior motive? If you read Matthew up to this passage in Chapter 12, you'll see that Jesus had done plenty of miracles. It wasn't as if they'd never seen Him do anything supernatural.

Some of them may have asked Him because they hated Him and wanted to discredit and destroy Him. Jesus said in the Sermon on the Mount, in Matthew Chapter 5-7, *"...except your righteousness shall exceed the righteousness of the scribes and Pharisees, ye shall in no case enter into the kingdom of heaven."* *(Matthew 5:20)*

He said that in public. Talk about politically incorrect! Can you imagine the looks on their faces when they heard that! No doubt some snarled, "How dare He say that!" And they were determined to destroy

Him. Others among them may have been unsure, and maybe even heard the Pharisees arguing among themselves whether Jesus was the Christ.

When they asked Him for a sign, He could have said, "You want signs? Look at the sick people I've healed, the dead I've raised, the devils I've cast out." But He, being God, knew their thoughts. He was not trying to win arguments. He was trying to win souls.

He looked past the sneaky motives of some of them and the uncertainty of others. He gave them the answer they needed IF they'd take heed to it and IF they were honestly seeking the truth. And this answer came from the source they already had: Scripture.

He referred to the book of Jonah in the Old Testament. He said that Jonah's time in the whale's belly was a preview of Jesus' time in the grave before rising again. In a nutshell, the Lord's basic answer to them was, "If you want a sign from God, look in God's Word."

John the Baptist was in prison at this time and sent two disciples to ask Jesus if He were the Messiah. Maybe John's faith was a little shaky. Ever feel that way? Maybe it's kind of encouraging to see that you're not alone.

Anyway, Jesus gave him the answer he needed. His answer, in part, was, *The blind receive their sight, and* *the lame walk, the lepers are cleansed, and the deaf hear, the dead are raised up, and the poor have **the gospel preached to them**." (Matthew 11:5, boldface added)*

The boldface is added to the last part because Jesus' most important reason for coming to earth was to die for sins, be buried, and rise again. That's a description of the gospel. He came most importantly so people could receive Him as their Saviour and have forgiveness of sins and eternal life.

You deal with so much sin and wickedness as a cop. Did you ever want a sign from God that He's still in control? Don't wait for lightning or a booming voice from heaven. God gave us a reliable and detailed sign that He's very real and very much in control. That sign is the Bible.

He also gave a promise that those who are honestly seeking Him will find Him: *"And ye shall seek me, and find me, when ye shall search for me with all your heart." (Jeremiah 29:13)* When you need to hear from God, take time to open your Bible.

Really, We're Nice Guys! by Patrick Evans

"A soft answer turneth away wrath:" (Proverbs 15:1)

In 1992, I was assigned to the Violent Fugitive Task Force. It was, as the name implies, a multi-agency task force with one mission: to locate and apprehend the most violent and dangerous fugitives. Our task force was made up of federal, state, and local law enforcement officers skilled in undercover operations and the use of specialized weapons and advanced tactics. This type of training was important since each environment would be unique and require mission-specific skill sets.

We trained as a unit and honed our collective skills in everything from CQB's (close quarter battle skills) and high-risk building entries to weapons and tactical countermeasures. We trained at the FBI Academy in Quantico, Virginia and the Camp Perry Military Installation near Port Clinton, Ohio. We trained hard and often in order to operate efficiently and successfully in the chaotic environments we'd face.

Constant, extensive training meant constant success. Yet for as great as the training was, it had one important shortcoming: it couldn't prepare us to deal with the emotional aftermath that our enforcement activities would have on the community.

When criminals are distinguished by their behavior as "violent fugitives", they need to be dealt with as such. Shock and overwhelming force are the oft-proven way for cops to deal with them. Unfortunately, criminals being what they are, they often hide among— and expose to risk--good people: men, women, and even children. THAT'S a problem because when officers have to apprehend them under these circumstances, things can get ugly.

A flash-bang grenade tossed into a house during a 4:00 AM hard-target search for a dangerous fugitive doesn't discriminate between innocent people and wanted murderers. It is an equal opportunity terrorizer.

A Task Force team storming into a suspect's house, ordering "EVERYONE!" to the floor at gun point and securing them until all threats are neutralized and the suspect is in custody has the same effect. These are great tactics for successful fugitive capture, but they don't help foster good relationships between the cops and the people we're sworn to protect and serve.

Aside from the fact that fugitives put them into these dilemmas to begin with, innocents are caught by no fault of their own between us and the dangerous people we're trying to apprehend. A loud explosion jarring you out of bed at 4:00 AM, followed by a bunch of armed strangers bursting in, screaming at you to get face down on the floor, then zip tying your hands behind your back doesn't give you a warm and fuzzy feeling about the cops. It does the opposite. It makes you fear them. Then fear turns into hate.

Yes, we got our fugitive, but at what cost? We did so at the expense of eight terrified innocents in the house. It's a terrible emotional price to pay, and it's especially bad when children are amongst that eight.

We realized that quickly snatching the fugitive out of the house and just leaving without saying another word was not a good option. At the end of the day, a tactical advantage is no advantage at all if you leave collateral emotional damage in its wake. And make no mistake about it, emotional damage counts.

Here is where Christian cops have an advantage. We know that police work is a ministry. *Romans 13:1* says, *"Let every soul be subject unto the higher powers. For there is no power but of God: the powers that be are ordained of God."* *Psalm 82:3-4* also fits our mission to protect and serve: *"Defend the poor and fatherless: do justice to the afflicted and needy. Deliver the poor and needy: rid them out of the hand of the wicked."* Yet the Owner's Manual ALSO tells us in *Romans 13:3, "For rulers* [people in authority; in this case, cops] *are not a terror to good works, but to the evil."*

We felt the responsibility, then, not only to apprehend the fugitive but also to de-terrorize the innocent people in the house. To that end, we developed a simple protocol. Two task force guys would transport the fugitive to jail while a couple of us would stay at the house and help calm everyone down. We found we made a huge difference when we took time to be sure everyone was all right and let them voice their feelings about what they'd just been through.

Often, they would scream and curse at us and cry. That was OK, and we let them know that it was OK. After they calmed down and were ready to listen to us, we would explain why we made the entry as we did.

We would also apologize for scaring them-- especially the kids. We would not leave the house until we were satisfied that everyone was OK (or at least as OK as you can be after something like that!)

They were still shaken up a bit but taking the time to explain really helped them understand WHY we sometimes have to make entries like that. When they realized that we did what we did for our safety AND THEIRS (lying on the floor gave them a tactical advantage in case the bullets started flying), their stress levels were greatly reduced.

Also, they always seemed to appreciate how we hung around, talked with them, and showed we cared about how they felt. We made it a point to try never to leave without a handshake or a high-five. So, I learned never to underestimate the power of an apology.

Do You Want to be Great?

"But the angel said unto him, Fear not, Zacharias: for thy prayer is heard; and thy wife Elisabeth shall bear thee a son, and thou shalt call his name John."

"For he shall be great in the sight of the Lord,"

"And many of the children of Israel shall he turn to the Lord their God." (Luke 1:13, 15, 16)

Zacharias and his wife Elisabeth had wanted a child, but she could not conceive. Now they were old. One day the angel Gabriel appeared to him and said, *"Fear not, Zacharias: for thy prayer is heard; and thy wife Elisabeth shall bear thee a son, and thou shalt call his name John."* The angel was talking about John the Baptist.

Obviously, Zacharias had been praying for a child, because Gabriel said his prayer had been heard. We don't know if Zacharias had still been praying, or if he'd given up after so many years. Yet God heard and answered his prayer with a child who would be not just "great", but *"great in the sight of the Lord"*.

No doubt you've heard of "great" people. Sonja Henie was a great figure skater. Harry James was a great trumpet player. Johnny Unitas was a great quarterback. Muhammad Ali was a great boxer. All were great in their own right, but earthly greatness is temporary.

1 Peter 1:24 says, *"For all flesh is as grass, and all the glory of man as the flower of grass."* Henie, James, and Unitas were big names in their day, but young people now may not even know who they were.

Why was John the Baptist *"great in the sight of the Lord"*? Because he chose to be used of God to bring people to Christ: *"And many of the children of Israel shall he turn to the Lord their God."* As a result of John's preaching, many would turn to Christ and be saved. That's the big difference between earthly greatness and being *"great in the sight of the Lord"*. Earthly greatness has no value beyond the grave.

Henie, James, Unitas, and Ali were great at what they did, but no one received Jesus as Saviour because of their earthly greatness. Being *"great in the sight of the Lord"*, however, has eternal value. God described John in this way because He wants us to be "great in his sight", too.

Sharing Christ with needy sinners is a work that's *"great in the sight of the Lord."* It's a work that's wise: *"...he that winneth souls is wise." (Proverbs 11:30)* It's also a work that lasts forever: *"And they that be wise shall shine as the brightness of the firmament; and they that turn many to righteousness as the stars for ever and ever." (Daniel 12:3)*

If you know Jesus as Saviour, please get this: police work is important, but it won't matter in eternity how many arrests you made, tickets you wrote or awards you received. It will matter what you did to reach others with the gospel.

You may never have the fame of some "great" person, but witnessing for Jesus is far more important and *"great in the sight of the Lord"*. Long after earth and its honors are gone, people God has used you to reach for Christ will be rejoicing with the Lord and with you in heaven.

Mickey Mantle was a great baseball player but a heavy drinker. His teammate Bobby Richardson was a born-again Christian. He spoke several times with Mantle about Jesus, but Mantle didn't seem to take him seriously.

Mantle was diagnosed with cancer one day. He called Richardson and asked for prayer. Near the end of his life, Mantle received Jesus as his personal Saviour. Mantle may have been a "great" baseball player, but Richardson's work of sharing Christ was and is far more important, and *"great in the sight of the Lord."* (info taken from "Mickey Mantle's 11th Hour Miracle" by James L. Lambert)

A Game of Life and Death

"Be sober, be vigilant; because your adversary the devil, as a roaring lion, walketh about, seeking whom he may devour: Whom resist stedfast in the faith,"
(1 Peter 5:8-9)

One day a police academy instructor confronted a recruit about unsatisfactory paperwork. The instructor yelled at him in front of other recruits, then threw the paperwork and made the recruit pick it up: classic boot-camp harassment.

Was the instructor being unfair? Absolutely, but he had a good reason. He was training the recruit to keep his cool under stress.

As a cop, you have to be ready for unfair situations. If you get into a fight against someone larger and younger, that's not fair. If a criminal attacks first or if you're in a gunfight against multiple assailants, that's not fair, either.

Yet that's police work. It's often not fair. It's not a game. No referees, no Marquis of Queensbury rules, as one training officer once said. Your opponent is often sneaky and vicious, and he plays for keeps.

When you stop a traffic violator and he starts to whine about you harassing him, he may be reaching for a gun at the same time, so you'd better watch his hands.

When you're on duty as a cop, you need to be sober and vigilant. It doesn't mean that you're not drunk (obviously, you shouldn't be), but that you're paying attention to what's going on about you.

Good guys have defeated bad guys many times in the past, and they'll do the same many times in the future, but the good guys have to be alert, because Cops and Robbers can be a game of life and death.

Paul said in *1 Timothy 6:12, "Fight the good fight of faith,"* It's called the good fight of faith for a reason. The Christian's *"good fight of faith"* and the police officer's fight against crime are similar in a way.

In the opening of his letter, Peter tells his readers that they are *"Elect according to the foreknowledge of God the Father, through sanctification of the Spirit, unto obedience and sprinkling of the blood of Jesus Christ:"* *(1 Peter 1:2)* So these are saved people.

Near the end of his letter he warns his readers—and by extension, us—*"Be sober, be vigilant; because your adversary the devil, as a roaring lion, walketh about, seeking whom he may devour:"*

When you have Jesus as your Saviour, you no longer have to wonder if you'll get to heaven. The Lord Jesus promised, *"And I give unto them eternal life; and they shall never perish, neither shall any man pluck them out of my hand." (John 10:28)* So the devil has lost your soul. Yet he can still "devour" Christians, which is why the warning to *"Be sober, be vigilant;"* is there.

You probably know cops who, in all honesty, don't do the cause of police work much good. Maybe they've had bad experiences (who hasn't?), or maybe they've just become lazy and uncaring. In a sense, they've been "devoured." Other cops, though, may have many years on and still love the job.

One way to stay enthusiastic for the job is to be sober and vigilant. Take it seriously. Another is to resist the urge to be lazy. Stay in shape. Keep your shooting and tactics sharp. Learn how to do your job better.

Be sober and vigilant in your Christian life, too, to avoid being devoured. Be alert for temptation, as well as for opportunities to share your faith in Christ.

Resist the devil *"...stedfast in the faith,"* too. Resist the urge to neglect your Bible, skip church, put off prayer, or let sin get a hold in your life. The devil, the ultimate criminal, is sneaky and vicious, but by God's grace, you can live a life that pleases God and that He uses to draw others to Him.

Someone you Can Trust

"Trust in him at all times; ye people, pour out your heart before him: God is a refuge for us. Selah." *(Psalm 62:8)*

God is everywhere. *Psalm 139:7* says, *"Whither shall I go from thy spirit? or whither shall I flee from thy presence?"* We're always in His presence, but when you know Jesus as Saviour, there's a sense of refuge that God gives when you take time to read His Word and pray.

When you read the Bible, think about what you're reading. *1 Timothy 4:15* says to *"Meditate upon these things;"* that is, the things from the Bible. Don't just plow through it. That's like cheating when you do pushups. When you cheat, you defeat the purpose of doing pushups. When you read the Bible thoughtfully, you can better catch things that the Lord uses to touch your heart.

Our verse says, *"Trust in him at all times;"* As a cop, you know what it means to trust someone. When you're in the passenger seat of a patrol car as your partner speeds lights-and-siren through traffic to a call or in a pursuit, you're literally trusting him or her with your life. If you're doing a building search on a burglary call, you're trusting other cops to help you if you find a suspect hiding inside.

In the same way and even more so, you can always trust the Lord, even on the job. Most police calls aren't handled in a cut-and-dried manner. Some are, but many involve judgment calls: "Should I enforce the law strictly, or cut some slack? If I handle this a certain way, how could it turn out?" In times like these, it's a good idea to pray quietly for wisdom. *Proverbs 2:6* says, *"For the LORD giveth wisdom:"*

You may already have a good idea how to handle a matter, but it's always a good idea to pray, anyway. *Proverbs 3:5* says, *"Trust in the LORD with all thine heart; and lean not unto thine own understanding."*

You might pray something like, "Lord, I have an idea how to handle this, but if I need to do something differently, please guide me." It can amaze you how God answers prayer and strengthens your faith.

You don't have to pray long or even out loud. God can see what you're dealing with. Just a brief, quiet request to God to give you guidance. A man named Nehemiah did that. His boss, King Artaxerxes, saw that he was sad. Nehemiah told him it was because Jerusalem was torn down. Here's what happened next:

"Then the king said unto me, For what dost thou make request? So I prayed to the God of heaven. And I said unto the king, If it please the king..." (Nehemiah 2:4-5)

When the king asked Nehemiah what he wanted, he had to answer right away, so his prayer had to be quiet and not take more than a second or two, maybe something like, "Lord, please help me with what to say."

Dave Pochatek and I pulled over a violator one day for an illegal turn. He had no license, but when we took him out of the car, we saw he had "boo-coo" money lying at his feet. We figured he was dealing drugs, but we had to find the drugs. If we didn't, we'd have to give him back the money: $6691, to be exact.

We put him into the patrol car. I checked his car prior to the tow. As I did, I was praying like this: "Lord, if he's got drugs, please let me find them." As I searched, I pulled out the ashtray and looked in the space underneath. I saw a small pouch inside. *Cool.* I got excited.

I pulled it out and opened it. I found several bags of powder inside. *See you later, $6691.* Dave was in the patrol car and saw me pumping my fist. I love stories with happy endings. Make it a habit to pray for wisdom and help on the job, even if your prayer is brief.

Obedience unto Death

"And Abraham said, My son, God will provide himself a lamb for a burnt offering:" (Genesis 22:8)

Abraham and Sarah wanted a child, but Sarah was barren. God promised one day that they'd have a son, and eventually Isaac was born. Later on, God gave Abraham a test. He told Abraham to sacrifice Isaac.

Abraham no doubt was sad at this command, but this was the same God who had saved him, given him the son, and answered many of his prayers and worked powerfully in his life. Abraham obeyed.

As they neared the mountain where the sacrifice would take place, Isaac asked, *"Behold the fire and the wood: but where is the lamb for a burnt offering?" (Genesis 22:7)* Abraham replied, *"My son, God will provide himself a lamb for a burnt offering:"*

When they reached the place, Abraham built an altar and laid wood on it. Then he took a rope and tied up Isaac. Now Isaac knew HE was to be the sacrifice! Abraham laid him on the altar on the wood. Then Abraham took a knife to kill his son, and that's where God stopped him.

This was an obedience test for Abraham and for Isaac. Isaac was about fourteen years old. Abraham called him a "lad," telling his servants, *"...I and the lad will go yonder and worship," (Genesis 22:5)*

Abraham's son Ishmael by Hagar, the Egyptian servant girl, was also called a "lad." God had told Hagar, *"Arise, lift up the lad* [Ishmael]*, and hold him in thine hand;" (Genesis 21:18)* At the time God said that, Ishmael was about fourteen years old. That's how we can figure that Isaac was about fourteen at the time of the sacrifice.

The best commentary on Bible verses is other Bible verses. That's why *1 Corinthians 2:13* talks about *"...comparing spiritual things with spiritual."*

When Abraham started tying up Isaac and Isaac realized what was about to happen, he could have bolted, but didn't. Here's another tactical point: when you tell a guy to turn around and put his hands behind his back, he knows the cuffs are coming out, so be ready in case he tries to bolt.

Glenn Jason and I had a young guy on a traffic stop. I was about to put him into the car when he suddenly broke away. I started to chase him on foot. He ran across the street and over a hill, out of sight. Glenn drove the car around the hill and also out of sight. I continued on foot in the same direction. A few seconds or so later, I heard the *pow* of a single gunshot.

Oh, no.

I ran over the hill. Glenn had the kid on the ground.

"I'm shot!" the kid cried. "I'm shot!"

"He's not shot," Glenn told me. "I shot in the air." The kid wasn't shot. We took him to jail.

At court time, he was convicted of some low-level misdemeanor. Glenn wasn't there, just me. The judge asked if he had anything to say before she passed sentence. He said, "I was scared and I ran and I heard the shot..." When he said, "I heard the shot," she smirked. So did the defense attorney. I stood there and tried not to look guilty. *Thanks, Glenn.*

Back to our story again: this story of Abraham and Isaac is a preview of Jesus' death on the cross. Abraham represents God the Father, giving His Son. Isaac represents Jesus, being willing to die.

Abraham said, *"...God will provide himself a lamb..."* and that's what God did. If anyone needs proof of God's love for people, Jesus' death on the cross is proof. *John 3:16* says, *"For God so loved the world, that he gave his only begotten Son, that whosoever believeth in him should not perish, but have everlasting life."*

Jesus is the central character of the whole Bible, not just the New Testament. Even in the Old Testament we find previews of what Jesus would do for us.

You're There for a Reason

"...who knoweth whether thou art come to the kingdom for such a time as this?" (Esther 4:14)

In the book of Esther, the Persian King Ahasuerus held a party, got drunk, and told his lovely wife Vashti to come and show her beauty. She refused. One of his advisers recommended that he dismiss her, which he did. Later he held a contest to choose his next wife. Esther, a young Jewish lady, won and became the queen of Persia.

Esther's cousin Mordecai had adopted her after her parents died. Mordecai was also a servant to Ahasuerus. One day Mordecai discovered a plot to assassinate the king. He told Esther. The plotters were hanged. Mordecai's deed was written in the king's chronicles.

The king later promoted Haman, a wicked, self-centered man, above the king's servants. They were to bow and reverence him, but Mordecai, a Jew, refused. Haman not only wanted Mordecai destroyed but all the Jews in the kingdom. He fast-talked the king into signing off on a decree that on a certain day, all Jews were to be killed.

Mordecai told Esther to plead to the king for her people. She was afraid to because she could be executed for going in without permission, but he told her, *"...who knoweth whether thou art come to the kingdom for such a time as this?"* Esther was scared but she agreed, saying, *"...so will I go in unto the king, which is not according to the law: and if I perish, I perish."* (Esther 4:16)

She went in. The king was glad to see her. She asked that he and Haman come to a banquet she'd prepared. They both came. At the banquet she asked them to come to a second banquet the next day.

Haman was excited at this star treatment, but told his wife, *"Yet all this availeth me nothing, so long as I see Mordecai the Jew sitting at the king's gate."* (Esther 5:13) Mrs. Haman replied, *"Let a gallows be made of fifty cubits high, and to-morrow speak thou unto the king that Mordecai may be hanged thereon:"* (Esther 5:14)

That night, the king couldn't sleep. He had the book of records of chronicles read to him. Maybe they were good reading for sleep. But he heard the story of Mordecai exposing the assassination plot. He asked if Mordecai had gotten a reward. His servants told him he hadn't.

Meanwhile, Haman was waiting in the outer court to see the king and ask him to have Mordecai hanged. The timing was perfect. The king called him in. Before Haman could say anything, the king asked, *"What shall be done unto the man whom the king delighteth to*

172

honour?" (Esther 6:6)

Haman was so stuck on himself, he thought the king was talking about him! He told the king that such a man should be paraded through the street on the king's horse, wearing the king's apparel and crown, and be honored publicly.

Imagine the shock on Haman's face when the king told him to do that honor to Mordecai! Haman had made it no secret that he hated Mordecai, so parading him around like that had to be a riot to watch. But it gets even better.

Later, at Esther's second banquet, she pleaded to the king for her life and that of her people because of an enemy that wanted to destroy them. Ahasuerus became angry and demanded to know who this enemy was. Esther pointed out Haman, who was sitting nearby. Things were getting worse for Haman by the minute.

The king was furious, and *"...in his wrath went into the palace garden:" (Esther 7:7)* Maybe he had to get his thoughts together after learning how wicked the adviser he trusted really was. Meanwhile, Haman got up to plead for his life and fell onto the bed where Esther lay. The king walked back in. What do you think was going through his mind when he saw Haman on his wife's bed?

You guessed it! He asked, *"Will he force the queen*

also before me in the house?" (Esther 7:8) As the saying goes, you could stick a fork into Haman because he was DONE! In the end, Haman was hanged on the very gallows that he had prepared for Mordecai.

God is never mentioned in this book, but His hand is obvious throughout the story. It all happened after one young lady did the right thing in a tough spot. Like Esther, you may find yourself in some tough spot where you don't want to be. But maybe it's no accident. Maybe God has you there to honor Him and make a difference *"...for such a time as this?"*

Choosing Your Battles

"Giving no offence in any thing, that the ministry be not blamed:" (2 Corinthians 6:3)

Police work is an offensive job by its nature. Cops do offensive things. They write tickets, run warrant checks, and arrest people. All these things are necessary, but for obvious reasons, they're likely to offend people. If you can avoid being offensive, you should at least try.

John Thomas was the first field training officer I worked with on a two-man car. He gave me an important piece of advice: never run a man down in front of his kids. I recall saying that to a young officer later when I was a sergeant.

If you go to a domestic fight and the father is involved, you're in his territory. Yes, you're the police, but if you talk down to him and make him look small in front of his kids, you're almost forcing him to fight just so he won't lose face. As much as it's possible to do, talk decently to people so you won't give offense needlessly.

Some pro athletes—not many, but some—have refused to stand for the National Anthem at games. The practice also seems to be losing popularity. Good.

Allegedly the protesters' issue is not with the Anthem

175

but with the actions of police officers. The protesters may never take the time to learn what police work is really like or how much people depend on them, including people in the inner city; but that's another issue. The point is that people in the public eye protest by not standing for the National Anthem.

Now even if their motives are honest, are they really calling attention to "bad cops"? Do people see them and think, "We need to do something about bad cops so these protesters will stand up"? Not likely. Even people who support them may say they have a right to protest like that. As a result, the focus is not on the supposed issue, which is bad cops, but on the protesters themselves.

Or are the protesters needlessly creating an offense and calling attention to themselves instead of the issue that they're supposedly protesting about?

Many people love the National Anthem. Protesters may say they mean no disrespect to anyone, but their protest is seen as an offense to men and women who've served, fought, and died for the rights we enjoy as Americans. By the way, if there were a Russian, Chinese, or North Korean NFL, it'd be interesting to learn what happens to players there who won't stand for the national anthem.

Dealing with people in crisis is hard enough. When people are in a crisis, they may say and do things they ordinarily wouldn't. Don't make things worse by being needlessly offensive.

If you're saved, the same principle is true, as our opening verse says. As a Christian, you should share the gospel, as the Lord said to do: *"Go ye into all the world, and preach the gospel to every creature." (Mark 16:15)* As you do, though, you'll meet people who don't like to hear that they're sinners who need to be saved from eternal hell. *1 John 3:13* says, *"Marvel not, my brethren, if the world hate you."*

People may not hate you enough to want to kill you, but once you talk with them a little and they learn that you're "one of those people" and you start "talking religion", people tend to take offense.

People can have preconceived notions that born-again Christians are judgmental, mean-spirited, holier-than-thou, phony, and unkind. The best way to fight those notions is to be kind, gracious, and inoffensive as you can be. *Colossians 3:12* says, *"Put on therefore, as the elect of God, holy and beloved, bowels of mercies, kindness, humbleness of mind, meekness, longsuffering;"*

Striving to be kind and gracious will go far to help you get past the initial offense and share Christ with needy people.

In for the Long Run

"... Moreover the man Moses was very great in the land of Egypt, in the sight of Pharaoh's servants, and in the sight of the people." (Exodus 11:3)

The Hebrews were held in slave-bondage in Egypt. God told Moses to go before Pharaoh and demand their release. Pharaoh not only refused, but he made their job harder. He told them to find straw to make brick on their own, but the daily quota of bricks would stay the same. They had to do more with less. Sound familiar?

Then when they didn't meet the quota, Pharaoh had them beaten. He abused them, just because he had the power. Do you know people like that on the job, bosses or patrol officers, who mess with people just because they can? Don't ever use power to mess with people just because you can, like Pharaoh did.

Moses was God's man. At first Pharaoh didn't take him seriously. On Plague #1, God turned the water to blood. The sorcerers of Egypt replicated this plague.

On Plague #2, God sent frogs to cover the land. Then Pharaoh took notice. He asked Moses to ask God to take away the frogs and he'd let the Hebrews go. Moses agreed, and the frogs died. Then Pharaoh went back on his word and wouldn't let the Hebrews go.

Plague #3 was lice. The sorcerers told Pharaoh, *"This*

is the finger of God:" (Exodus 8:19) Interestingly, they knew there was a true God and they were serving false gods. When they said, *"This is the finger of God:"* Pharaoh's heart was hardened. People will sometimes harden their hearts when God is dealing with them.

Sometimes Pharaoh would ask for respite, but when God gave it, Pharaoh would go back on his word. God sent plagues of lice, flies, murrain (livestock disease), and boils. While Pharaoh played games with God's judgment, though, others in Egypt watched Moses.

Moses warned Pharaoh about Plague #7: *"Behold, tomorrow about this time I will cause it to rain a very grievous hail, such as hath not been in Egypt since the foundation thereof even until now." (Exodus 9:18)* The hail would wipe out the crops and kill every person and beast. Look at what happened when word got around! Even Pharaoh's servants took Moses seriously!

"He that feared the word of the LORD among the servants of Pharaoh made his servants and his cattle flee into the houses:" (Exodus 9:20)

People in Egypt saw that Moses didn't quit. They saw that he was in for the long run and they respected him.

If you're saved, the most important thing you can do in life is to witness for Christ. That's what the Great Commission—*"Go ye into all the world, and preach the gospel to every creature." (Mark 16:15)*--is about.

It often isn't easy to stand for Christ as a cop, but don't quit. Moses didn't quit when things got tough. He hung in and gained experience. You'll gain experience by arrests, uses-of-force, and other things cops do.

You'll also gain Christian experience as you stand for Christ as a cop. You'll learn how to talk about the Lord with people. You'll learn to pray and look for chances to witness, even in a small way. You'll learn to watch your personal conduct, so as not to be a bad testimony. You'll learn to be thick-skinned if people give you a hard time.

As you serve the Lord, He can give you grace to care about people and not develop a toxic attitude as cops sometimes do: *"And the Lord make you to increase and abound in love toward one another, and toward all men,"* *(1 Thessalonians 3:12)*

If you serve the Lord as a cop, you'll see Him work through your life, too. You won't see plagues like in Egypt. Those were special miracles for a special time. But you'll provoke people's thinking, and the Lord will open doors for you to witness for Christ to them.

The Egyptians learned to take Moses seriously. People on the job will learn to take you seriously when they see you're consistent. Consistency builds credibility.

All About Me

"I have seen all the works that are done under the sun; and, behold, all is vanity and vexation of spirit." (Ecclesiastes 1:14)

When Solomon wrote Ecclesiastes, he obviously wasn't happy. He'd put his faith in the Messiah, he was rich, and he was wise. But he wasn't happy. Listen to his words:

"I made me great works; I builded me houses; I planted me vineyards: I made me gardens and orchards, and I planted trees in them of all kind of fruits: I made me pools of water, to water therewith the wood that bringeth forth trees:" (Ecclesiastes 2:4-6)

Take a look at that passage again. Solomon kept using a certain word; five times in this passage, to be exact: "ME" "ME" "ME."

Yet he said in *Ecclesiastes 2:11, "Then I looked on all the works that my hands had wrought, and on the labour that I had labored to do: and, behold, all was vanity and vexation of spirit, and there was no profit under the sun."* In eternal terms, all his work was a big waste of time.

Solomon's problem was that he was living "under the sun." He used that phrase several times in the book of Ecclesiastes. To live "under the sun" is to go through the functions of earthly life that people go through.

No doubt many people today live "under the sun." They eat, drink, work, play, raise kids, and go on life's way; all of which isn't sinful, but it has no eternal value.

Early in his reign, *"...Solomon loved the LORD, walking in the statutes of David his father:" (1 Kings 3:3)* So how did Solomon go from being on fire for the Lord to the spiritual rut of his later life? One big mistake was hanging out with the wrong people:

"But King Solomon loved many strange women, ...Of the nations concerning which the LORD said unto the children of Israel, Ye shall not go in unto them, neither shall they come in unto you: for surely they will turn away your heart after their gods: Solomon clave unto these in love. And he had seven hundred wives, princesses, and three hundred concubines: and his wives turned away his heart. For it came to pass, when Solomon was old, that his wives turned away his heart after other gods: and his heart was not perfect with the LORD his God, as was the heart of David his father." (1 Kings 11:1-4)

Solomon hung out with heathen people, then fell in love with and married heathen women, in direct disobedience to God's warning. As a result, his heart was turned away from God, which is exactly what God had said would happen. People are much better off if they just take God at His Word.

If you know Jesus as Saviour, you have forgiveness of all your sins forever and a home in heaven when you die. Many people would love to have assurance like that and don't, but you do. You also have the most important purpose in the world: to share the gospel of Jesus' death, burial, and resurrection and salvation with lost people.

Yet how is your heart toward God? Do you care about pleasing Jesus and telling others about Him? Are you happy serving the Lord in a Bible-believing church? Or are you just living "under the sun" in life's rat race?

If you're "under the sun" and honest enough to admit it, look at whom you hang out with. They DO influence you, whether or not you realize it. Do they encourage you to live for the Lord, or tend to turn your heart from Him as Solomon's heathen "friends" did to him? Are your friends good cops but a bad spiritual influence? If you're around people who are a bad influence, you know it.

Don't be content to live "under the sun." One day you'll see Jesus face to face. You don't want to look back on your life and see how little you did for Christ, and how many chances to witness were wasted because you were too occupied with your heathen "friends." You don't want your life to be "all about me."

Jesus Loves Even Me-and Them, Too

"And should not I spare Nineveh, that great city, wherein are more than sixscore thousand persons that cannot discern between their right hand and their left hand; and also much cattle?" (Jonah 4:11)

Jesus said, *"For as Jonas was three days and three nights in the whale's belly; so shall the Son of man be three days and three nights in the heart of the earth." (Matthew 12:40)* We know the story of Jonah and the whale is a true story because Jesus said it was. It also has some great spiritual lessons. Let's look.

God had told Jonah to go to Nineveh and warn the people of God's judgment, but Jonah didn't want to go. He boarded a ship to flee from God. God sent a storm.

The sailors on the ship worshipped different false gods, and when the storm rose, they *"...cried every man unto his god," (Jonah 1:5)* The false gods couldn't do anything to help. After all, they were *false* gods. Then the sailors threw out some of the cargo. That didn't help, either.

The captain found Jonah asleep and told him to pray so they wouldn't perish. When they learned Jonah worshipped *"...the LORD, the God of heaven," (Jonah 1:9)* and that Jonah was running from Him, they were even more afraid and asked Jonah what they should do.

He knew the storm was because of him, so he told them to throw him overboard. They didn't want to do that at first, but they eventually did, asking God to forgive them. Right away the sea was calm. The sailors became worshippers of the true God. Lesson 1: don't run from God. Lesson 2: God wants to save people. He may even use crazy circumstances to do it.

Then along came the whale. *"Now the LORD had prepared a great fish to swallow up Jonah. And Jonah was in the belly of the fish three days and three nights." (Jonah 1:17)*

God told the whale to vomit Jonah up. Then God told Jonah—again--to go to Nineveh. Jonah went this time; not that he suddenly cared about the Ninevites, but he probably didn't want another trip into the whale's belly. Jonah did the right thing this time. Maybe his motive wasn't the best, but he did the right thing.

Lesson 3: Do the right thing, even if your motive isn't the best. For instance, don't skip church if you're able to go. *Hebrews 10:25* says, *"Not forsaking the assembling of ourselves together,"* Even if you go just to say you went, which isn't a good reason, God may use the preaching to speak to your heart about some issue in your life, and you're glad you went.

Jonah went to Nineveh and preached, *"Yet forty days, and Nineveh shall be overthrown." (Jonah 3:4)* God touched the hearts of the king and all the people. They repented of their wickedness, and God spared them.

Jonah told God, *"...I knew that thou art a gracious God, and merciful, slow to anger, and of great kindness, and repentest thee of the evil." (Jonah 4:2)* Jonah even asked, *"Therefore now, O LORD, take, I beseech thee, my life from me; for it is better for me to die than to live." (Jonah 4:3)* Jonah wanted to die.

God didn't kill Jonah. God asked him, *"Doest thou well to be angry?" (Jonah 4:4)*

Jonah was in a lousy mood. Ever felt like that? God dealt with Jonah's heart in just the right way. Lesson 4: When you're in a lousy mood---which can happen on this job--open your Bible and trust God to speak to your heart through *"...the voice of his word." (Psalm 103:20)* Tell Him how you feel, as Jonah did.

God pointed out that the Ninevites had souls. The phrase *"...cannot discern between their right hand and their left hand;"* may have been about small kids, or about people with no spiritual discernment, no knowledge of God.

As a cop, you often see people, even small kids, in filthy, sin-laden, dysfunctional homes with little if any sense of God-fearing, stability, or love. Yet here's Lesson 5: Like the Ninevites, there's no one the Lord Jesus isn't willing to forgive and save.

Triggered!

"They angered him [God] also at the waters of strife, so that it went ill with Moses for their sakes: Because they provoked his spirit, so that he spake unadvisedly with his lips." (Psalm 106:32-33)

When you're a cop, people may try to provoke you with words, because they know they can. They know that you're held to a higher standard, and if you do or say something in the heat of emotion, it's likely to be caught on your body camera.

It's also likely to be recorded on the smartphones that are probably recording. In fact, some people may purposely provoke you and record the event hoping to catch a bad reaction for evidence in a lawsuit.

"Cyberbaiting" is purposely provoking someone to anger and secretly recording the incident as it's going on in order to publicize it. Some people obviously have nothing better to do with their time.

Did you ever hear the saying, "An idle mind is the devil's workshop and idle hands his tools"? People may do things like this because a) they're criminals or they sympathize with criminals and don't like cops; or b) lawsuit settlements are an easier way to get money than working an honest job.

Under the badge, you're human. Bible characters

were human, too. Some of them had bad moments that cost them. Moses had a bad moment that cost him.

God had used Moses to do mighty things: the plagues in Egypt, the parting of the Red Sea, and many miracles in the wilderness. Unfortunately, the Israelites had a bad habit of complaining. Time and again they'd complain and wish they were back in Egypt.

Their complaining caused Moses a lot of stress. He even told God, *"And if thou deal thus with me, kill me, I pray thee, out of hand, if I have found favour in thy sight;"* (Numbers 11:15)

At one point, there was no water for the people to drink. They started to complain again about not being in Egypt. They'd obviously forgotten how cruelly the Egyptians had treated them. The devil used their complaining to provoke Moses to anger, as our verse says.

God told Moses to speak to a rock, and it would give water. Instead, Moses said, *"Hear now, ye rebels; must we fetch you water out of this rock?"* (Numbers 20:10) Then he hit the rock twice with a rod. They provoked him so that he *"spake unadvisedly with his lips."*

First, *"we"*—God and Moses, that is—didn't provide water. God provided the water. Only God deserved the credit, not Moses. Second, he was supposed to speak to the rock, not strike it. No doubt Moses was stressed out because of all their complaining, but God still held Moses accountable for his actions. Because of what he'd done, Moses was not allowed to lead the Israelites into the Promised Land.

God also pointed out the Israelites' sin in provoking Moses. Provocation is a form of temptation. Paul told the Christians at Thessalonica, *"...lest by some means the tempter* [the devil] *have tempted you," (1 Thessalonians 3:5)* The devil uses *means* to tempt people to sin. Sometimes the means he uses is people.

So when someone on the street "provokes your spirit, so you're tempted to speak unadvisedly with your lips", and you want to hit him like Moses hit the rock (but don't), remember he's being used of Satan to provoke you to sin, like the devil used the Israelites to provoke Moses. Think of the devil standing behind the guy taunting you, egging him on, and he's following the devil's lead.

If you see another officer in a situation like that, step in to help. The devil may try to use a loud-mouth suspect to provoke the officer, but you can be used of God to help him. You may end up saving another officer from a bad moment that will cost him.

Truth Stands

"And ye shall know the truth, and the truth shall make you free." (John 8:32)

When someone lies to you, it's sometimes obvious. Say you're called to an auto theft at 3:00 a.m. at a gas station in a bad area. The victim says his car was stolen at gunpoint. When you learn he lives in a distant suburb, you'll probably suspect he rented out his car for drugs, and the renter is past his return time.

If you ask why he's in the area at this time, and he says something like, "I was buying cigarettes", you might ask, "Don't you have all-night gas stations closer to home?"

If you just make an armed robbery report, though, for what's actually a drug rental, some cops may see the car rolling later and think the driver is an armed robber. The driver/renter may see police cars behind him and speed off in a panic because he has a warrant, he's got "a little bit of weed," he knows the car is reported stolen, he has no license, or any combination of these.

A high-speed chase could follow, which could get ugly. That's why you need to get the truth, even if your victim is embarrassed. It will come out eventually. The sooner it does, the better for everyone involved.

Ever hear that the biggest problem in police work is

the "disconnect between the police and the communities they serve"? That's a convenient line for people who want to make the police the bad guys, but it's flatly not true.

Yes, some cops could use a personality check. Others may say or do something stupid in the heat of emotion. Still others may blunder outright, and some officers may be outright bad apples, but the worst problem in police work is not some "disconnect." Crime doesn't happen because of some "disconnect."

The worst problem is criminals: they burglarize, rob, sell drugs, steal cars, drive recklessly, make life hard for decent people, make cities unattractive, and fight and sometimes kill cops. Criminals are and have always been the main problem in police work.

2 Corinthians 13:8 says, *"For we can do nothing against the truth, but for the truth."* Truth will always stand against lies. Evolutionists can scoff at the idea of God, but it's still true that *"In the beginning God created the heaven and the earth." (Genesis 1:1)*

Even Jesus verified creation: *"...**he which made them at the beginning** made them male and female, And said, For this cause shall a man leave father and mother, and shall cleave to his wife:" (Matthew 19:4-5, boldface added)*

It's also true that God gives life in the womb, no

matter what the seven Roe v. Wade yes-votes said in 1973: *"Thus saith the LORD that made thee, and formed thee from the womb," (Isaiah 44:2)* It also doesn't matter that five Supreme Court justices approved same-sex marriage. God ordained marriage for a lifetime for *"...male and female,"*

Nor does it matter that people are now being recognized as "transgender," or that the Fed at one time had threatened to withhold money if public schools didn't make bathrooms gender-neutral. God's truth still stands that people are *"...male and female,"*

Lies are not kind. Lies don't help people. Truth must be told; told kindly, but it must be told. People need to be told that they're sinners headed for hell, but that Jesus, God the Son, died for their sins, was buried, and rose again. This is God's truth. Jesus said, *"I am the way, the **truth** [boldface added], and the life: no man cometh unto the Father, but by me." (John 14:6)*

People may not want to hear that they need to repent of sin and come to Christ, but the sooner they receive the truth, the better. Once they stop fighting God and receive Jesus as Saviour, something wonderful happens. Their entire sin-debt is forgiven, and they have Jesus' indwelling presence forever and a home in heaven to look forward to. Then it happens to them as Jesus said: *"And ye shall know the truth, and the truth shall make you free."*

The Best Thing About Heaven

"For the Lord himself shall descend from heaven with a shout, with the voice of the archangel, and with the trump of God: and the dead in Christ shall rise first: Then we which are alive and remain shall be caught up together with them in the clouds, to meet the Lord in the air: and so shall we ever be with the Lord. Wherefore comfort one another with these words." (1 Thessalonians 4:16-18)

This Scripture tells about Jesus' Second Coming. No one knows when He'll return, but He's assured us He will. He'd also said before His death that He'd rise again, and many people didn't believe that, but He did.

Likewise, as wild as it sounds, we see in this passage that Christians who are alive will be caught up to heaven: *"...we which are alive and remain shall be caught up together with them in the clouds, to meet the Lord in the air: and so shall we ever be with the Lord."*

Heaven is a beautiful place. The world's most beautiful places can't compare to the beauty of heaven: *"But as it is written, Eye hath not seen, nor ear heard, neither have entered into the heart of man, the things which God hath prepared for them that love him." (1 Corinthians 2:9)*

Heaven is also a holy, sinless place: *"And there shall in no wise enter into it any thing that defileth, neither whatsoever worketh abomination, or maketh a lie: but they which are written in the Lamb's book of life."* *(Revelation 21:27)*

In heaven, there will be no robbers, auto thieves, drug dealers, or gangs terrorizing citizens. The crime rate will be absolute zero. In patrol, you've probably had occasional slow shifts where the adrenaline junkies almost want something to happen. In heaven, though, people will enjoy the fact that it's so peaceful and perfect. They will *"...delight themselves in the abundance of peace." (Psalm 37:11)*

The greatest thing about heaven, though, is this: *"...and so shall we ever be with the Lord."* It doesn't say, "and so shall we be in a beautiful place", or "and so shall we be in a holy place," or "and so shall we be free of trouble and sorrow", although all these are true.

It says, *"...and so shall we ever be with the Lord."* We'll be in the presence of Jesus Himself. We'll see Him and bow down and worship Him and thank Him personally for being our Saviour:

> *"Heaven for me it will be Heaven for me.*
> *Jesus will be what makes it Heaven for me.*
> *All its beauty and wonder I'm longing to see, but*
> *Jesus will be what makes it Heaven for me."*
> *"(Jesus Will be What Makes it) Heaven for Me",*
> *Words and Music by Lanny Wolfe*

It will be a joyful time, but also a very serious time. It will be a time when we give account to the Lord at the Judgment Seat of Christ.

"...we shall all stand before the judgment seat of Christ." (Romans 14:10)

We won't be judged for our sins. Our sins were already judged on Jesus' cross! But we will be judged on what we did to serve Him and reach lost people with the gospel:

"So little time! The harvest will be over.
Our reaping done, we reapers taken Home.
Report our work to Jesus Lord of Harvest,
And hope He'll smile and that He'll say,
"Well done!"
"So Little Time" by John R. Rice

Christian, God has given you time and resources to help people escape eternal hell. Yet one day your time will end, and you'll account to the Lord for how you used the time and resources He let you have. Please decide right now to be a faithful witness for Christ, while you can!

"And now, little children, abide in him; that, when he shall appear, we may have confidence, and not be ashamed before him at his coming." (1 John 2:28)

Jesus Loves the Little Children

"And they brought young children to him, that he should touch them: and his disciples rebuked those that brought them. But when Jesus saw it, he was much displeased, and said unto them, Suffer the little children to come unto me, and forbid them not: for of such is the kingdom of God. Verily I say unto you, Whosoever shall not receive the kingdom of God as a little child, he shall not enter therein. And he took them up in his arms, put his hands upon them, and blessed them."
(Mark 10:13-16)

Many people came to see Jesus, including parents with kids. But when they tried to get close, the disciples turned them away! "Hey, take these kids away! Jesus is too busy for a bunch of kids!" No doubt the kids and parents were sad at not being able to see Jesus.

Jesus saw what His disciples had done. He was *"...much displeased,"* He stopped what He was doing, checked his disciples' error, and put whatever He was doing on hold while He spent some time with kids.

Young kids are great because they're honest. We were called to a domestic one evening. The man of the house had allegedly struck the woman. I saw a little girl there, maybe four years old. I took her aside and asked, "Honey, did daddy hit mommy?" She nodded her head up and down in exaggerated, little-kid fashion.

I told the man, "Your daughter says you hit the lady." He acted surprised, turned to her and asked, "Did daddy hit mommy?" Again, she nodded up and down.

Once on church visitation I stood at the door of a house. A boy about eight years old who obviously lived there stood nearby. I told the lady I was visiting from church. She politely replied, "Well, we have a church and we go every week." Then the boy piped in, "No, you don't!"

Jesus loves everyone, but He has a special affection for kids. He knows how innocent and vulnerable they are. He said, *"But whoso shall offend one of these little ones which believe in me, it were better for him that a millstone were hanged about his neck, and that he were drowned in the depth of the sea." (Matthew 18:6)* That's a serious warning for anyone who would corrupt a child.

We see that Jesus not only endorses the death penalty, but even said that it's better for the offender; not better for society, but for HIM! How could it be better for him? The biggest reason would be that he'd have a chance to receive Jesus as Saviour before the execution.

The worst thing that could happen to anyone is not death, but death without Christ, and God is *"...not willing that any* [not even those who'd entice children to sin] *should perish* [go to hell for eternity]*, but that* *all* [even they] *should come to repentance."* (2 Peter 3:9)

Unfortunately, kids can grow up in sinful environments. As Bob Cerba and I rolled past a group of kids one evening, we heard a kid's high-pitched voice swear at us. We stopped the car and got out.

We weren't going to do anything official—what were we going to do, arrest a little kid for swearing? But it seemed a good learning moment and a chance to do some public relations. We asked who'd said that. A small boy said without hesitation that he had.

We asked him, "Do you know what that meant, what you said?" He looked right at us and shrugged. He had no idea. An older kid had probably told him to say that as the police passed by, and the older kid had probably heard it from people older than him.

If you know Jesus as Saviour, never write off kids. Never look at kids in a bad environment and think there's no hope. They have souls, and Jesus loves them just as much as He loved the kids in the story. They may have plenty of bad influences, but *1 Corinthians 15:58* says, *"...your labour is not in vain in the Lord."*

Anything you do to reach them for Christ is never a waste. If you can touch a kid's life, even with a small kind word or deed, do it. God can take that little bit you do and turn it into a chance to share the gospel of Christ.

Rejoicing in the Truth

"Now the God of hope fill you with all joy and peace in believing, that ye may abound in hope, through the power of the Holy Ghost." (Romans 15:13)

God is *"the God of hope."* The hope He gives is a good hope, a sure hope. He gives us joy and peace as we believe His Word, trusting His Word as truth.

Picture a little kid at a third-story window of a burning house. Outside the window beneath him are eight big, strong firefighters holding a safety net, yelling for him to jump. They can catch him and save him, but he has to *believe* on them, to accept their offer of salvation as truth, and jump. If he does, he'll be saved. If he doesn't, he'll perish in the flames.

That's how you come to Jesus. You accept God's truth that you've sinned and are separated from God: *"For all have sinned, and come short of the glory of God;" (Romans 3:23)* And that your sins have condemned you to death and hell: *"For the wages of sin is death;" "And death and hell were cast into the lake of fire." (Romans 6:23, Revelation 20:14)*

You also accept that God the Son, Jesus Christ, died on the cross to pay your sin-debt, was buried, and rose again: *"...Christ died for our sins according to the scriptures; And that he was buried, and that he rose again the third day according to the scriptures:" (1*

Corinthians 15:3-4) "Who his own self bare our sins in his own body on the tree," (1 Peter 2:24)

Finally, you come to the risen Jesus in repentance, trusting Him entirely (believing) to forgive and save you when you receive Him: *"...him that cometh to me I will in no wise cast out." (John 6:37) "But as many as received him, to them gave he power to become the sons of God, even to them that believe on his name:" (John 1:12)*

Once you receive Jesus as Saviour, you can accept as truth God's promise that Jesus has forgiven and saved you: *"...He that believeth on me hath everlasting life." (John 6:47)* He's God. He cannot lie.

God also has many more promises for believers than that. *2 Peter 1:4* says, *"Whereby are given unto us exceeding great and precious promises:"* Once you know Jesus as Saviour, you have many promises in His Word you can accept as truth. The more you read His Word, the more promises you'll find to trust and rejoice in, the better you know Jesus and see His love for you, and the more your love for Him grows.

You'll be tempted at times not to believe His Word. For instance, God promised, *"...I will never leave thee, nor forsake thee." (Hebrews 13:5)* But if things aren't going well in your life, you may think God has forsaken you. You may neglect your Bible, skip church, and become angry at God. That's easy for a cop to do.

200

Don't do it. Don't trust your circumstances. Trust God's promises. God made promises. He meant them. You can trust God's Word.

Do you feel your faith is weak? That can happen. The remedy to lack of faith is God's Word: *"So then faith cometh by hearing, and hearing by the word of God."* *(Romans 10:17)* This verse isn't just for lost people to come to Christ to be saved. It's also for saved people to grow in their faith.

Grace for Danger

"Who through faith...out of weakness were made strong, waxed valiant in fight, turned to flight the armies of the aliens." (Hebrews 11:33-34)

Police work is dangerous. That's easy to forget if you've never done police work or have any connection to cops and you listen to the wrong people.

Flying lights-and-sirens to a "man with a gun" call, for instance, zigzagging through traffic, is dangerous and scary. You try to pass people and they won't pull over, either because they're knuckleheads or they're in their own little world, blasting their music.

Once you're on scene, looking for the armed suspect is also dangerous and scary, especially after dark. You poke into dark places with a flashlight and gun. Most of the time you don't have good cover. Your suspect may be watching you, even if you don't see him. You don't want to shoot him, but he may be willing to shoot you to avoid being arrested.

If you find him but you can't see empty hands, you still have a problem. You may yell, "SHOW ME YOUR HANDS!" If he doesn't, you may yell several times more. Why keep yelling, and not just shoot? Because you don't want to shoot if you can avoid it.

Of course, he may fumble with his hands, refusing

your orders. Is he hiding drugs? Reaching for a gun? Or just being an idiot? If you think he's pulling a weapon and you shoot him but there's no weapon, you'll be the star of the nightly news for a long time to come. But if he has a gun and shoots you, there will be one less cop to protect the citizens and one still-healthy and still-dangerous criminal to prey on them.

If you want to walk this thin blue line, you need courage. If you're a cop and you've trusted Jesus as Saviour, you can trust the Lord by His grace to give you courage, as our opening passage says.

Goliath was bigger, better-armed, and more experienced than David. Yet David gave God the glory and trusted God to give him the victory. He told Goliath, *"And all this assembly shall know that the LORD saveth not with sword and spear: for the battle is the LORD's, and he will give you into our hands." (1 Samuel 17:47)*

David fought many battles in his life, and testified how the Lord gave him strength for battle:

"For by thee I have run through a troop; and by my God have I leaped over a wall. As for God, his way is perfect: the word of the LORD is tried: he is a buckler to all those that trust in him. For who is God save the LORD? or who is a rock save our God? It is God that girdeth me with strength, and maketh my way perfect. He maketh my feet like hinds' feet, and setteth me upon

203

my high places. He teacheth my hands to war, so that a bow of steel is broken by mine arms. Thou hast also given me the shield of thy salvation: and thy right hand hath holden me up, and thy gentleness hath made me great. Thou hast enlarged my steps under me, that my feet did not slip. I have pursued mine enemies, and overtaken them: neither did I turn again till they were consumed. I have wounded them that they were not able to rise: they are fallen under my feet. For thou hast girded me with strength unto the battle: thou hast subdued under me those that rose up against me." (Psalm 18:29-39)

This passage is great to hang up in your locker and read before you hit the street, or better yet, commit to memory and remind yourself of God's promise of courage when you need it.

Still the Best Policy

"And Abram journeyed, going on still toward the south. And there was a famine in the land: and Abram went down into Egypt to sojourn there; for the famine was grievous in the land. And it came to pass, when he was come near to enter into Egypt, that he said unto Sarai his wife, Behold now, I know that thou art a fair woman to look upon: Therefore it shall come to pass, when the Egyptians shall see thee, that they shall say, This is his wife: and they will kill me, but they will save thee alive. Say, I pray thee, thou art my sister: that it may be well with me for thy sake; and my soul shall live because of thee.

And it came to pass, that, when Abram was come into Egypt, the Egyptians beheld the woman that she was very fair. The princes also of Pharaoh saw her, and commended her before Pharaoh: and the woman was taken into Pharaoh's house. And he entreated Abram well for her sake: and he had sheep, and oxen, and he asses, and menservants, and maidservants, and she asses, and camels. And the LORD plagued Pharaoh and his house with great plagues because of Sarai Abram's wife. And Pharaoh called Abram, and said, What is this that thou hast done unto me? why didst thou not tell me that she was thy wife? Why saidst thou, She is my sister? so I might have taken her to me to wife: now therefore behold thy wife, take her, and go thy way. And Pharaoh commanded his men concerning him: and they sent him away, and his wife, and all that he had." (Genesis 12:9-20)

Abram (whom God would later call Abraham) was about seventy-five years old. His wife Sarai (later to be known as Sarah) was sixty-five. A famine was in the land. Abram took Sarai and all his property and people and went into Egypt, where there was food.

As they neared Egypt, Abram worried that the Egyptians would see how pretty Sarai was and kill Abram so they could have her. Abram didn't know that they would do this, but he was afraid of what might happen, so he thought up a lie to avoid trouble.

Sure enough, the Egyptians saw how beautiful she was, and Pharaoh took her into his own house. He also gave Abram servants, sheep, oxen, and other animals.

Yet God stepped in and plagued Pharaoh's house because of Sarai. Pharaoh found out the truth, and confronted Abram. He'd thought, and logically so, that because Sarai was Abram's sister, that she was available for marriage.

Abram lied to avoid something he didn't know would happen. As a result, he set up his wife to be defiled by another man, he brought plagues upon innocent people, and he brought reproach on God. Abram would have been better off telling the truth to begin with.

Abraham was greatly used of God, yet in this case, he was in the wrong. Lying isn't ok because Abram did it, any more than drunkenness is ok because Noah did it or adultery is ok because David did it. When we read in the Bible of a servant of God sinning, we see that he is an imperfect character. We also see the terrible results that sin brings, in the lives of the sinner and the lives of innocent people.

When you're a cop, times will come when you're tempted to lie on the job, times when "no one" knows the truth. Yet God knows. Let integrity be your guide: *"The integrity of the upright shall guide them:" (Proverbs 11:3)* Lying may seem a good idea, but as we see in this instance, it doesn't turn out well. If you're saved, honesty pleases God and is a good testimony for Christ: *"Lying lips are abomination to the LORD: but they that deal truly are his delight." (Proverbs 12:22)*

Racial Equalizer

"For there is no respect of persons with God."
(Romans 2:11)

Imagine a call like this: *"Any car able to respond, we have a report of a burglary in progress. The victims are a black couple in their 60's."* Or maybe, *"Radio to any car, a white store clerk is being robbed at gunpoint."* Wouldn't those be crazy? It doesn't matter what race the victims are. It only matters that they need your help NOW. So, you speed off to help them.

Race doesn't matter to good cops. Good cops do their best for victims of any race. Cops are often accused of mistreating minorities, yet on any violent-crime-in-progress call with non-white victims, it'd be interesting to see how many cops responded, each officer's race, how fast each one arrived, and what each officer did on the call that involved personal risk: a building search, a foot chase through yards, a fight with a suspect.

Stats like these will provide a more honest and thorough look at how cops perform. They'll also show clearly what cops and decent people already know: cops of all races put their lives on the line time and again for all people.

Race also doesn't matter to victims. When they're being robbed, their houses are being kicked in, they hear gunfire, or the drug dealer is walking up and down the street, they don't care so much if the cop who comes looks like them. They care that the cop gets there fast.

Race doesn't even matter to suspects. They don't care if the cop is the same color as they. Criminals only see a uniform. White cops have been shot and murdered by white criminals. Black cops have been shot and murdered by black criminals.

Racism can be a cheapshot accusation, like mud that's thrown in hopes it will stick. I'd been accused of racism; not often, but it has happened. If a motorist accused me of racism in connection with, say, a traffic stop, I'd cite him for the violation. Here's why:

He may just be trying to get out of the ticket, but he also may be trying to get money. If I let him go to show that "I'm not racist", he can sue me civilly. His lawyer would argue that I had no probable cause to pull him over and I only let him go because I knew he was right. In the process of trying to smooth a situation over, then, I've played into his hands.

Remember, this is America. People are innocent until proven guilty. I don't have to demonstrate that I didn't act in a racist way. The accuser has to demonstrate that I did.

Back to the main point: the sacredness of life is a great racial equalizer. I can't say how many high-risk calls I'd answered with white, black, Hispanic, Asian, and female cops. It's an adrenaline junkie's dream. We're doing something dangerous but important. We don't care about race or gender. We're all a team, focused on a goal that's bigger than any of us: helping a victim of violent crime and stopping a predatory suspect.

One night in roll call, Sgt. Arthur Armstrong was calling off names of patrol car crews. When he got to Kobylinski and Kornatowski (I'm not making these names up), he looked at one, called the other's name, then said, "White guys all look alike to me." Stan Kobylinski, by the way, was somewhat slim with glasses. Dave Kornatowski was husky, no glasses.

And speaking of "all you people look alike", Jerry Goode told me how he was talking with a citizen who suddenly asked him, "Hey, what happened to the last digit on your badge?" Jerry's badge was 58. Mine was 585. The citizen thought he was talking to me, which was interesting since Jerry stood about four inches shorter than me and was black.

The gospel of Jesus Christ is the greatest racial equalizer in the world. It puts all people on the same plane before God. Each of us is guilty of sin and separated from God as a result: *"For ALL have sinned, and COME SHORT of the glory of God;"* [capitals added] *(Romans 3:23)* Each of us is condemned to death and hell for sin: *"For the wages of sin is death;"* *"And death and hell were cast into the lake of fire."*

(Romans 6:23, Revelation 20:14)

Yet God the Son, Jesus Christ, took all our sins to His cross on Calvary: *"And that he died for ALL,"* [capitals added] *(2 Corinthians 5:15)* Jesus was buried and rose again! *"I am he that liveth, and was dead; and, behold, I am alive for evermore, Amen;" (Revelation 1:18)*

Jesus' offer of forgiveness and salvation is for all: *"But AS MANY AS RECEIVED HIM, to them gave he power to become the sons of God, even to them that believe on his name:"* [capitals added] *(John 1:12)* *"For WHOSOEVER shall call upon the name of the Lord shall be saved."* [capitals added] *(Romans 10:13)*

When any person of any race receives Jesus as Saviour, the same wonderful thing happens: the Lord gives the sinner eternal forgiveness of all sins, His indwelling presence, an eternal home in heaven, and the most important task in the world: to share this good news with people of all races.

Joy of Assurance

"He that hath the Son hath life; and he that hath not the Son of God hath not life." (1 John 5:12)

There are two kinds of people in the world: those who have the Son, who know Jesus as Saviour, and those who don't. Those who have Jesus have eternal life. Those who don't, don't. This verse isn't about earthly life. Even an atheist or devil worshipper has that. But when you've received Jesus as your personal Saviour, you have eternal life. The Bible says so.

When you have Jesus, you never have to worry that you won't go to heaven, because the Bible says, *"He that hath the Son hath life;"* Verses like this are in the Bible so people who've received Jesus as Saviour won't need to doubt if they'll get to heaven.

In fact, *1 John 5:13*, says, *"These things have I written unto you that believe on the name of the Son of God; that ye may **know*** [boldface added] *that ye have eternal life,"* So anyone who's received Jesus as Saviour can say, "I know I'm headed for heaven because I've received Jesus as my Saviour. The Bible says that anyone who's done that HAS eternal life!"

The Bible gives many assurance passages. Paul said in *Philippians 1:21*, *"For to me to live is Christ, and to die is gain."* He also talked about trials he faced as a Christian and said he had *"...a desire to depart, and to*

be with Christ; which is far better:" (Philippians 1:23)
How could he be so sure that when he died, he'd be in
heaven with Jesus? Because he'd accepted Him as
Saviour. Peter also said in *1 Peter 1:4* that believers in
Jesus have *"...an inheritance incorruptible, and
undefiled, and that fadeth not away,* **reserved in heaven
for you,** *"* (boldface added) Aren't those words of
assurance great?

Peter, Paul, and John said so, and even Jesus Himself
said to believers, *"...rejoice, because your names are
written in heaven." (Luke 10:20)* God doesn't want
people to be uncertain whether they'll go to heaven.
The Bible has these verses and plenty more to prove
that point.

1 John 4:18 says, *"...fear hath torment."* God
doesn't want people tormented with uncertainty about
eternity. That's why He inspired the writers to say what
they did. God wants people to enjoy the assurance that
they're headed for heaven.

Now some may ask, "Well, if I'm guaranteed to go to
heaven, why not just go hog-wild with sin?" Good
question. Here's the answer. God has given us His
Word, the Bible, to help us live right: *"Wherewithal
shall a young man cleanse his way? by taking heed
thereto according to thy word." (Psalm 119:9)*

Once you've received Jesus as your Saviour, you also
have something else: His permanent presence inside

213

you. Day and night, 24/7/365, and even when you're tempted, Jesus is with you and in you. *Galatians 2:20* says, *"...Christ liveth in me:"*

The Lord also says in *Hebrews 13:5, "...I will never leave thee, nor forsake thee."* Let that thought sink in. Once you receive Jesus as Saviour, He'll never leave or forsake you. Ever. His indwelling presence will also help you live for Him.

I was on St. Clair Avenue one night about 3 am. I saw a white guy driving with a Lake County (the next county east) license plate. I've worked long enough in high-crime black neighborhoods to know that when a white guy is in the area at 3 am and not in a police uniform, there's a good chance something's not right.

I followed him. His driving was perfect. He drove west on St. Clair to Eddy Road, turned right, then took Eddy to the I-90 entrance eastbound back toward Lake County. Whatever his reason was for being in the area, the presence of a person—specifically a person in a police uniform—helped him to act right.

Likewise, the indwelling presence of a person— Jesus--will help you "act right" in your Christian life, speak to your conscience about sin, and help you fellowship with Him and serve Him.

Why did This Have to Happen?

"Although thou [Job] *sayest thou shalt not see him* [God], *yet judgment is before him; therefore trust thou in him." (Job 35:14)*

You're on patrol. You get a domestic call. You pull up to the house. A woman flies out the front door. She's bloody and hysterical. Her boyfriend is inside the house with their son. You run in and go quickly from room to room, gun pointed. Your heart is pounding.

You get to the kitchen. A guy with a BIG meat cleaver has a little boy in front of him. You yell at him to drop it. He swears at you and says he'll kill the kid. You yell again. He won't drop it. You sight in at his chest, above the boy's head. You yell again.

He pulls the boy's head back. This is happening too fast. You yell for the millionth time. He puts the meat cleaver to the boy's throat like he's about to slit it. You fire. He drops. The knife falls. The boy screams. He's hysterical.

You pull the boy to safety, kick the knife away, and grab your collar mic: "Radio, send EMS. Officer-involved shooting, suspect down, everyone else OK." You're surprised at how calm you are.

You holster your gun and put on latex gloves. You put direct pressure on the dark, ugly blotch on his chest.

215

You talk to him. He stares past you at the ceiling, his eyes half-closed. You don't want him to die.

Someone takes the kid away. Then the post-shooting circus starts. Police cars fly to the scene. Crowds gather. EMS takes him away. The higher-ups arrive. TV cameras are outside. You hear later that he died.

No doubt you feel crummy. That doesn't mean you didn't do right. Don't trust emotions. They can deceive you. Instead, ask yourself two questions: 1) who could have been killed or injured if you hadn't done something? and 2) what other REASONABLE thing could you have done (key word: REASONABLE) with the same amount of knowledge and time to decide?

The boy may not understand all of what happened. He may ask, "I thought police were our friends?" "Daddy wouldn't hurt me. Why did the policeman shoot him?" "Why didn't the policeman just take the knife away?"

Hopefully mom will tell the truth in a simple way: *"daddy tried to hurt mommy and he tried to hurt you and the police came to help and they had to do what they did."* If he hears the truth, he'll more likely have peace of mind about it. But if people fill his head with lies, he may believe them and hate cops because he listened to lies.

You as an adult understand the shooting better than

the. God also understands everything far better than we do. *Isaiah 55:9* says, *"For as the heavens are higher than the earth, so are my ways higher than your ways, and my thoughts than your thoughts."*

Like the boy, we may not know why things happen in life. But as our opening verse says, we can trust God even in dark times. Job served God faithfully, but he had lost seven kids. If anyone had the right to ask God "why?", Job did. Yet Job even said of God, *"Though he slay me, yet will I trust in him:" (Job 13:15)*

What if the boy grows up and learns more about the shooting from a public records check? That's good. The more truth he gets, the more peace of mind he'll have. The records will give him truth and dispel lies.

God also gave us a public record—the Bible—to tell us the truth about Him and dispel lies. If you want to know about God, don't just look for a sign in the sky or listen to people who may not know what they're talking about. Look in His Word for answers! God promises us, *"And ye shall seek me, and find me, when ye shall search for me with all your heart." (Jeremiah 29:13)*

If you need assurance that God loves you, the best proof of God's love is the cross of Jesus. That's where God the Son loved you and paid your sin-debt: *"Hereby perceive we the love of God, because he laid down his life for us:" (1 John 3:16)*

Temptation on the Blind Side

"And Satan answered the LORD, and said, Skin for skin, yea, all that a man hath will he give for his life. But put forth thine hand now, and touch his bone and his flesh, and he will curse thee to thy face. And the LORD said unto Satan, Behold, he is in thine hand; but save his life. So went Satan forth from the presence of the LORD, and smote Job with sore boils from the sole of his foot unto his crown. And he took him a potsherd to scrape himself withal; and he sat down among the ashes. Then said his wife unto him, Dost thou still retain thine integrity? curse God, and die. But he said unto her, Thou speakest as one of the foolish women speaketh. What? shall we receive good at the hand of God, and shall we not receive evil? In all this did not Job sin with his lips." (Job 2:4-10)

Satan had already gotten God's permission one time to bring disasters into Job's life. Satan thought Job would curse God to His face after all the disasters, but Job didn't. Next, Satan asked God's permission to touch Job's health.

This passage describes the second meeting. God gave him permission. The devil gave Job a whole-body case of boils. With the loss of his children, plus the pain he was now in, no doubt he was tempted to turn his back on God already. Then Mrs. Job came along. She was no help.

In fairness to Mrs. Job, though, she'd been married to him all this time and mothered his ten children. She'd also seen how he loved and served God faithfully, and she'd probably had a decent walk with the Lord, too; at least until that time.

Moreover, when the first round of disasters came, she was hit by them, too. She had lost seven kids, too. She'd lost all that property and all those servants, too. In all likelihood, she wasn't standing there laughing at him at all. She was probably in a terrible emotional state, and as most cops know, people can say and do unwise things when they're in a bad emotional state.

Here's another important lesson: when you're going through a tough time on the job, you can be sure your spouse is feeling it, too. Police spouses have extra loads to carry that most spouses don't, so they deserve whatever extra love and consideration you give them.

Debbie and I were sitting in Sunday School one time. As the teacher talked about the awfulness of sin in its various forms, he commented on how terrible it would be to kill someone.

I doubt anyone else in the room caught it, but Debbie and I both did. We weren't offended, and I'm sure he didn't mean to offend. In a way, it was kind of funny. Still, his words struck a chord with us. Debbie turned to me and said quietly, "We'd been through that." Not "*you'd* been through", but "WE'D been through."

Anyway, Mrs. Job surely wasn't trying to be a tool of temptation, but she was. We see then that the devil can even use people close to you, whom you love and respect, to tempt you to sin.

The temptation to *"curse God, and die"* was probably stronger coming from Mrs. Job than it would have been coming from a stranger. Yet even coming from her, Job didn't respond to the temptation with sin.

If someone you love says something sharp or unkind, it's worse than a stranger saying it, but no matter where the temptation is coming from, you don't need to respond with sinful words. It's not God's fault that your loved one is having a bad moment. Don't we all have them? Christians, and even preachers, can have bad moments. Noah, David, Peter, and other Bible heroes had bad moments.

Or if someone in church acts in an un-Christian way, don't quit church. Even Christians can say and do wrong things for whatever reason, but that's not Jesus' fault. Don't sin against the Lord because of what others do. Temptation can come from many unexpected sources. Just keep your focus on *"...Jesus the author and finisher or our faith;" (Hebrews 12:2)* He'll help you when it does.

The Greatest Power for the Greatest Good

"For I am not ashamed of the gospel of Christ: for it is the power of God unto salvation to every one that believeth; to the Jew first, and also to the Greek." *(Romans 1:16)*

Jesus said, *"For what shall it profit a man, if he shall gain the whole world, and lose his own soul?" (Mark 8:36)* So the most important possession a person has is his soul, and the best info a person can get in his life is how to be sure of going to heaven.

If you know Jesus as Saviour, you know that the best news you ever heard was the gospel: that Jesus died for your sins, was buried, and rose again. You also know that the best decision you ever made was to receive Jesus as your Saviour.

Now that you have Jesus as Saviour, you're God's child: *"For ye are all the children of God by faith in Christ Jesus." (Galatians 3:26)* You have forgiveness for all your sins: *"...whosoever believeth in him shall receive remission of sins." (Acts 10:43)* You have Jesus' indwelling presence: *"...Christ in you, the hope of glory:" (Colossians 1:27)*, and His promise of eternal life: *"...He that believeth on me hath everlasting life." (John 6:47)*

At one time, though, you didn't have Jesus. You weren't a child of God, you didn't have forgiveness of your sins, or Jesus' indwelling presence, or any hope of heaven. You were condemned to death and hell for your sins: *"He that believeth on him is not condemned: but he that believeth not is condemned already," (John 3:18) "For the wages of sin is death;" "And death and hell were cast into the lake of fire. This is the second death." (Romans 6:23, Revelation 20:14)* But someone shared the gospel of Christ with you. Aren't you glad someone wasn't ashamed to tell you about Jesus?

Well, just as God sent someone to you, God wants to send you to those who don't know Jesus--who are still where you used to be--and share the gospel: even other cops. That idea may sound scary, but the Lord said, *"Go ye into all the world, and preach the gospel to every creature." (Mark 16:15)* He didn't say to wait until they came to us. He said to go to them. If you are saved, then, God has you where you are to witness for Christ to others, even other cops.

Of course, your first job is to do police work. The Lord even said, *"Render therefore unto Caesar the things which are Caesar's;" (Matthew 22:21)* Of all people, Christians should be good workers. How you do your job can help you be a good testimony for Christ, an *"...epistle...known and read of all men:" (2 Corinthians 3:2)*

People watch you. When you work hard and strive to treat people decently, even when they're difficult, you show people that Jesus is Somebody real, Somebody important to you. A good testimony will help you when you get an opportunity to witness for Christ later.

No, you're not paid to witness, but cops also talk about everything under the sun: sports, other cops, bosses, dispatchers, politics, you name it. Even on a busy shift, you can also have some down time.

If you don't know if your partner knows Jesus, pray for a chance to share Christ and not be ashamed. When an opening comes, you can give a gospel tract from your church, if you go to a church where the Bible is preached and where people hear how to be saved (why would you go to any other kind of church?).

You can also say something simple, like, "May I give you an invitation to our church? We like to give out invitations. It also has some Scripture about heaven you may enjoy." Very short and simple.

That's one easy way to share the gospel. Sharing Christ may be scary at first, but the more you do it, the less scary it is. Look for ways to show care and compassion to people, including cops, and ask the Lord to give you openings and ways to witness and grace not to be ashamed. Don't ever be ashamed of Jesus.

Thanks, I Needed That!

"Faithful are the wounds of a friend;"
(Proverbs 27:6a)

An after-shave commercial long ago said that the product wakes you up like a cold slap in the face. In the ad, a man is slapped in the face and says, "Thanks, I needed that." In a way, that's one idea of this passage. Sometimes people need a "cold slap in the face" to see the error of their ways.

What if you had a close friend who was addicted to alcohol or gambling? People who like to drink and gamble may argue that these behaviors don't always enslave people. That's true, but it's also true that doing either of them is playing with fire. *Proverbs 6:27* says, *"Can a man take fire in his bosom, and his clothes not be burned?"* You may not become a drunk or a problem gambler, but your son or daughter who follows your example might.

What of your friend with the problem, though? Gambling and alcohol are expensive (and sinful) habits. He may be in money trouble as a result. Does he spend a lot of time at the bar or casino, or buy multiple lottery tickets? Yes, those are gambling. Does he work excessive part-time, probably trying to recoup his losses? If he has a wife and kids, you can be sure they're hurting too, but he probably won't tell you.

What do you do? Wait until he kills himself, gets divorced, or is fired? He's hurting himself, his family, friends, and even you. You need to look him in the eye and tell him to stop before he destroys himself and innocent people. It won't be fun, but you need to a be a faithful friend who "wounds" him and sets him straight.

If you see a cop taking needless risks at work that may get him or others hurt, what do you do? What if he gets himself into danger and other cops risk getting hurt or killed trying to help him, which you know they will?

You need to "wound" people like that and set them straight before something bad happens. If you're uneasy telling him yourself, tell a boss. You're not a snitch. You could be saving cops' lives.

As a boss, sometimes you have to "wound" subordinates who look sloppy, aren't doing their job, or are doing things they shouldn't. When you do, of course, it should be in private. Always praise officers in public and correct them in private. Your problem officer may not like to hear it, but it's better coming from you in a private chew-out session than from the Complaint Unit or Internal Affairs.

Even as a boss, I've been put in my place by patrol officers plenty of times. One night I helped a patrol crew handle a break-in call. I pulled up first and scouted the house from next door, in the backyard. It was quiet.

The patrol car pulled up. I told the crew I'd scouted it out. Nick Przybylski (pronounced shi-BIL-ski) sat in the driver's seat and looked up at me over the top of his glasses. He didn't say a word. He just looked. The longer he looked, the more uncomfortable I got.

Truth to tell, I knew better than to do what I'd done. If two or three bad guys had come out the back door with guns, I'd have been in a serious trick bag.

Another time, I had a traffic stop. Robin Vontorcik was dispatching. I gave her the license plate info, then stepped out and did the stop. She was going to give me the listing, but I didn't wait. I had done plenty of traffic stops, so I knew everything.

Nothing happened on this one, but afterward, she talked with me—or rather, AT me—over the phone. She was upset. I caught the edge in her voice.

"Why didn't you wait for the listing? What if he'd had a warrant?" I had no good reason not to wait. I was just being a cementhead while she tried to watch my back. As one lieutenant said, "a good dispatcher is like gold" and Robin is a good dispatcher.

If you're a parent, you have to chastise your kid when he misbehaves. It's not fun, but you do it because you love him and want him to stop the bad behavior. How many youngsters have you seen on the job who don't act right, and they obviously weren't raised right?

God, being a loving Father, chastens His children at times: *"For whom the LORD loveth he correcteth; even as a father the son in whom he delighteth."* *(Proverbs 3:12)* If you're saved but having problems, it may not be because of sin in your life, but it may be. Pray and ask God, *"Search me, O God, and know my heart: try me, and know my thoughts: And see if there be any wicked way in me,"* *(Psalm 139:23-24)*

Don't let pride blind you. If someone "wounds" you as a faithful friend, tell him later, "Thanks, I needed that." *Hebrews 12:11* says, *"Now no chastening for the present seemeth to be joyous, but grievous: nevertheless afterward it yieldeth the peaceable fruit of righteousness unto them which are exercised thereby."*

If God deals with you about sin, it's not fun. If you confess and forsake it, though, then you can say, *"I know, O LORD, that thy judgments are right, and that thou in faithfulness hast afflicted me."* *(Psalm 119:75)* You could even say, "Thank you, Lord. I needed that."

Pleasant Words

"Pleasant words are as an honeycomb, sweet to the soul, and health to the bones." (Proverbs 16:24)

Proverbs 21:19 says, *"It is better to dwell in the wilderness, than with a contentious and an angry woman."* As a cop, you've probably gone to domestic fights where no crime was committed, so you told the husband, or the "baby's father", to leave for a while and cool off. That's like the idea of *Proverbs 21:19*. If the woman is in a bad mood, the man needs to vacate, at least temporarily.

Now let's take *Proverbs 21:19* one step further. It not only tells the man to vacate when necessary, but it also indirectly tells the woman to do a personality check.

Let's say that whenever a man sees his wife getting into a "mood", he vacates to the gym, garage, or basement, anywhere away from her. If this happens often enough, maybe she'll eventually get the hint and try to be less of a *"contentious and an angry woman"* and more pleasant to be around.

Of course, men can be just as bad. David's men had an encounter with a man named Nabal and his wife Abigail. *1 Samuel 25:3* says that Abigail *"...was a woman of good understanding, and of a beautiful countenance: but the man* [Nabal, her husband] *was churlish* [cruel] *and evil in his doings;"* One of their servants even told Abigail that Nabal *"...is such a son of Belial* [a wicked person], *that a man cannot speak to him." (1 Samuel 25:17)* When a man tells his boss' wife what a jerk he is and she agrees, what does that tell you about him?

One main point of *Proverbs 21:19* is that God wants His people to speak pleasant words that are *"...sweet to the soul, and health to the bones."* You may have heard the saying, "Always be sure your words are sweet, in case you ever have to eat them."

Did you ever work with a partner who consistently griped and whined and badmouthed others? Chronic whining is a bad testimony for Christ. If you need help to be more pleasant (and who among us doesn't need that sometimes?), spend more time in God's Word. Pleasant words are sweet to the soul and health to the bones, and God's words are the most pleasant on earth: *"The statutes of the LORD are right, rejoicing the heart:" (Psalm 19:8)*

God's Word is pleasant to read and to think about. *Psalm 119:48* says to "meditate" (ponder on) God's Word: *"...I will meditate in thy statutes."* The more you read God's Word and commit it to memory, the more it will influence your thinking and speech.

Keep a small Bible handy, or even just a New Testament, especially one with Psalms and Proverbs. When you have down time, even only a few minutes, you can take time for God's Word instead of the newspaper or some dumb game on your phone.

Psalm 23 is a great Scripture for cops. Verse 4 says, *"Yea, though I walk through the valley of the shadow of death, I will fear no evil: for thou art with me;"* The phrase, *"the valley of the shadow of death"* refers to a place of danger. If you've been on the job for any length of time, no doubt you've spent time in some "valley of the shadow of death."

Yet if you know Jesus as Saviour, He's always with you. He even said, *"...I am with you alway, even unto the end of the world. Amen." (Matthew 28:20* He was and still is with you always. Isn't that great?

The more you read your Bible, the better you'll know your Saviour, and the more you'll love Him and want to fellowship with Him by reading His words which are sweet to the soul, and health to the bones.

Swallow Your Pride, Tough Guy!

"These six things doth the LORD hate: yea, seven are an abomination unto him: A proud look, a lying tongue, and hands that shed innocent blood, An heart that deviseth wicked imaginations, feet that be swift in running to mischief, A false witness that speaketh lies, and he that soweth discord among brethren." *(Proverbs 6:16-19)*

If you ever heard the phrase, "the seven deadly sins", here's where it came from. These sins aren't listed in order, like pride is worst, lying is second worst, murder is third, etc., but simply as seven things that God hates. Interestingly, pride is listed first. The Bible mentions many times how God hates pride:

"...pride, and arrogancy, and the evil way, and the forward mouth, do I hate." *(Proverbs 8:13)*

"Pride goeth before destruction, and an haughty spirit before a fall." *(Proverbs 16:18)*

Lucifer the angel wasn't satisfied to be a servant to God. He wanted to be like God. For his pride and rebellion, he and the angels who followed him were expelled from heaven for ever:

"How art thou fallen from heaven, O Lucifer, son of the morning!" *"For thou hast said in thine heart, I will ascend into heaven, I will exalt my throne above the*

231

stars of God: I will sit also upon the mount of the congregation, in the sides of the north: I will ascend above the heights of the clouds; I will be like the most High. Yet thou shalt be brought down to hell, to the sides of the pit." (Isaiah 14:12-15)

Job 41 describes a fearsome creature known as leviathan: *"...shall not one be cast down even at the sight of him?" (verse 9) "...his teeth are terrible round about." (verse 14) "...a flame goeth out of his mouth." (verse 21)*

Verse 34 says something interesting about the leviathan: *"....he is a king over all the children of pride."* That's a comparison of the leviathan to the devil, since a scaly monster doesn't hold authority over people.

The phrase, *"the children of pride"* obviously refers to people who have not received Jesus as Saviour and are still in their sin. A group of scribes and Pharisees started an ugly confrontation with Jesus. He told them, *"Ye are of your father the devil," (John 8:44)* Not that they were his biological offspring, but they were acting with his nature of rebellion against God.

No doubt pride is one reason some people don't receive Jesus as Saviour. People can be too proud to admit that they're sinners who need a Saviour. They may think their religion or personal goodness should satisfy God. They may worry what people will think if

232

they accept Jesus. That's also pride.

2 Kings 5:1-19 tells of Naaman, a Syrian military captain. He was a leper. His wife's servant was a Hebrew girl who'd been taken captive. She told Mrs. Naaman that Israel's prophet, Elisha, could cure Naaman of his leprosy. Naaman went to see Elisha, but Elisha didn't see him personally. He sent a messenger to tell him to wash in the Jordan River seven times.

Naaman was mad because Elisha didn't come to him personally. He also didn't want to wash in Israel's Jordan River. He wanted to wash in a Syrian river: *"Are not Abana and Pharpar, rivers of Damascus, better than all the waters of Israel? may I not wash in them, and be clean?"* (2 Kings 5:12) He was prideful because of his position and because of his nationality.

Too bad. Elisha had specified the Jordan, so Naaman could either obey or die a proud leper. Naaman was smart. He swallowed his pride and did as he was told.

Seven dunks in the Jordan later, the leprosy was gone. Naaman was thrilled. More important than the healing, he had a wonderful change of heart. He took Israel's God as his God and was saved.

Naaman was a tough guy, but the best thing he ever did was swallow his pride. You may be a tough cop, but if you know you need Jesus as Saviour, do what Naaman did: swallow your pride and receive

Him: *"...God resisteth the proud, and giveth grace to the humble." (1 Peter 5:5)* Come to Christ as a repentant sinner seeking forgiveness and let Him save you by His grace. A hundred years from now, you'll look back on that decision as the best you ever made.

God Wants your Heart

"Draw nigh to God, and he will draw nigh to you."
(James 4:8)

If you're a cop, life can be busy. There's your job, part-time job(s), court, and family. For a Christian on the job, it can be easy to let personal devotion time— Bible reading and prayer—go by the wayside.

In a way, it's like exercise. You know you need to do it, but you work crazy shifts, go into OT, and you may go from the job to part-time, or even from part-time #1 to part-time #2. By the time you get home, all you want to do is peel off the gear, shower, and crash.

It's easy to get out of the habit of working out, and into the habit of eating the wrong stuff and too much of it. You have to make a conscious effort at regular exercise, but it's worth the effort.

It's the same with personal devotion time. You can find time to do it, because there's always time for what is important, but you probably need to re-order your priorities a bit. You need to decide on purpose to spend time with God in His Word and prayer.

Our Scripture says, *"Draw nigh to God, and he will draw nigh to you."* As believers, we can either draw near to God and enjoy close fellowship with Him, or not. Yet God wants us to enjoy fellowship with Him, and He with us. That's why the verse is there.

You draw near to God by reading His Word. But don't just flip open your Bible and bla-bla-bla through some verses. Expect the Lord to speak to your heart. Pray like the psalmist said in *Psalm 119:18: "Open thou mine eyes, that I may behold wondrous things out of thy law."*

If you're a parent, you want your kids to obey, but you should also want the affection of their hearts, so don't just give orders and criticize all the time: "Clean your room." "Get off the phone." "Don't give me an attitude." You need to correct them at times, but you also need to encourage them with words of care, guidance, and love.

Isn't it awful, by the way, to be at a call and hear parents yell and swear at their young kids? That's a great way to lose a kid's heart. *Colossians 3:21* is in the Bible for a reason: *"Fathers* [and by logical implication, mothers]*, provoke not your children to anger, lest they be discouraged."* If a parent is verbally abusive, it's not hard to figure out why kids run away.

God also wants to have the hearts of His children: *"My son, give me thine heart,"* (Proverbs 23:26). God's Word isn't just a set of "Thou shalts" and "Thou shalt nots." Yes, the Bible has commands, but it also has words of hope, wisdom, instruction, and encouragement.

236

Psalm 19:7-8, for instance, says, *"The law of the LORD is perfect, converting the soul: the testimony of the LORD is sure, making wise the simple. The statutes of the LORD are right, rejoicing the heart: the commandment of the LORD is pure, enlightening the eyes."* When you have down time at work, open your Bible. You make better use of time, and if another cop sees you reading the Bible, God can use it as an opening to talk with him about Jesus.

Prayer is also part of "drawing nigh to God." *1 Peter 5:6-7* says, *"Humble yourselves therefore under the mighty hand of God, that he may exalt you in due time: Casting all your care upon him; for he careth for you."*

Do you have cares as a cop? Things that bother you about the job, or the department where you work? How about your family? All of us have cares. Do you have a friend you can confide in? One who's willing to listen and whom you can trust not to talk?

The Lord wants to be a friend like that, too. If you know Jesus as Saviour, don't just fret about your cares. Cast them on God in prayer, *"...for he careth for you."*

Better than Experience

"But Thomas, one of the twelve, called Didymus, was not with them when Jesus came.

The other disciples therefore said unto him, We have seen the Lord. But he said unto them, Except I shall see in his hands the print of the nails, and put my finger into the print of the nails, and thrust my hand into his side, I will not believe. And after eight days again his disciples were within, and Thomas with them: then came Jesus, the doors being shut, and stood in the midst, and said, Peace be unto you.

Then saith he to Thomas, Reach hither thy finger, and behold my hands; and reach hither thy hand, and thrust it into my side: and be not faithless, but believing. And Thomas answered and said unto him, My Lord and my God. Jesus saith unto him, Thomas, because thou hast seen me, thou hast believed: blessed are they that have not seen, and yet have believed." (John 20:24-29)

You've probably heard experience is the best teacher, and it usually is. It certainly is in police work.

After Jesus rose from the dead, He appeared to His disciples:

"Then the same day at evening, being the first day of the week, when the doors were shut where the disciples were assembled for fear of the Jews, came Jesus and stood in the midst, and saith unto them, Peace be unto you. And when he had so said, he shewed unto them his

hands and his side. Then were the disciples glad, when they saw the Lord." (John 20:19-20)

They may not have recognized Him at first. Mary Magdalene didn't recognize Him at first after His resurrection, either. Yet His first words to them were, *"Peace be unto you."*

Then He showed them the ugly wounds in His hands and side. There was no mistaking where He'd gotten them. They were thrilled to see Him, but "Doubting Thomas" wasn't there; and when the other disciples told him, he said he wouldn't believe it until he'd seen and touched the wounds himself.

The next time, the Lord answered Thomas' challenge directly, and invited him to *"Reach hither thy finger, and behold my hands; and reach hither thy hand, and thrust it into my side: and be not faithless, but believing."* Thomas didn't even take up the Lord's challenge. He was convinced, and said, *"My Lord and my God."*

Think of what Jesus said afterward: *"...blessed are they that have not seen, and yet have believed."* No one nowadays has seen Jesus as the apostles did. We know that no one has seen Jesus because *1 Peter 1:8* talks of Jesus, *"Whom having not seen, ye love;"* So if you hear a preacher say he's seen Jesus in a vision, now you know better. Either the Bible is wrong or he's wrong. Obviously, it's not the Bible.

Since we've never seen Jesus, though, how are we supposed to believe that there is a God and a Heaven and a Hell; and that Jesus, who is God the Son, died for our sins and rose again; and that He forgives and saves those who put their trust in Him, and that He wants us to tell others about Him and live pleasing to Him? Well, the Lord gave us something better experience that we can trust: He gave us the Bible.

Peter described a personal experience with Jesus in his second epistle, but he referred to the Scripture as *"...a more sure* [not equally sure, but MORE SURE] *word of prophecy;"* (2 Peter 1:19)

The more experience you have as a cop, the more you tend not to trust people. That's not wrong, since you often deal with people who shouldn't be trusted. Yet even as an experienced cop, you can enjoy a walk of faith with the Lord by spending time often in His Word. Spending time in God's Word will help strengthen your faith in the Lord: *"So then faith cometh by hearing, and hearing by the word of God."* (Romans 10:17)

One Celebrity

"And when he had taken the book, the four beasts and four and twenty elders fell down before the Lamb, having every one of them harps, and golden vials full of odours, which are the prayers of saints. And they sung a new song, saying, Thou art worthy to take the book, and to open the seals thereof: for thou wast slain, and hast redeemed us to God by thy blood out of every kindred, and tongue, and people, and nation; And hast made us unto our God kings and priests: and we shall reign on the earth.

And I beheld, and I heard the voice of many angels round about the throne and the beasts and the elders: and the number of them was ten thousand times ten thousand, and thousands of thousands;

Saying with a loud voice, Worthy is the Lamb that was slain to receive power, and riches, and wisdom, and strength, and honour, and glory, and blessing." *(Revelation 5:8-12)*

In the beginning of Revelation 5, John the Apostle sees God the Father on His throne holding a sealed book. No one is worthy to open it. John weeps. But then he hears the wonderful news!

"...the Lion of the tribe of Juda, the Root of David, hath prevailed to open the book, and to loose the seven seals thereof." (Revelation 5:5)

John continues to write,

241

"And I beheld, and, lo, in the midst of the throne and of the four beasts, and in the midst of the elders, stood a Lamb as it had been slain, having seven horns and seven eyes, which are the seven Spirits of God sent forth into all the earth. And he came and took the book out of the right hand of him that sat upon the throne." *(Revelation 5:6-7)*

The Lamb is Jesus, God the Son. *"Behold the Lamb of God, which taketh away the sin of the world." (John 1:29)* He is the Lamb because His sacrificial death on the cross at Calvary paid our sin-penalty before a holy God, and He was buried and rose again.

Now pick up to our passage. Look how much attention Jesus gets!

"Worthy is the Lamb that was slain to receive power, and riches, and wisdom, and strength, and honour, and glory, and blessing."

No one in heaven is thinking how hard he worked to get there. They all know they're in heaven and not hell entirely because of Jesus: *"...thou wast slain, and hast redeemed us to God by thy blood..."*

Some people are celebrities on earth: actors, musicians, pro athletes, people of power and influence. Do you have a favorite celebrity? What has he or she done for you personally? Could you call him or her on the phone? Probably not. They may be special to you, but you're not special to them. They may even be decent people; which hopefully, they are. Still, they're only human, and their celebrity status will one day be gone, like all things of earth: *"...for the things which are seen are temporal;"* *(2 Corinthians 4:18)*

In heaven, though, for eternity, Jesus will have everyone's attention, and He'll deserve it all! If you've trusted Jesus as Saviour, you know that He did for you what you couldn't do for yourself! Here on earth you can draw near to Him by reading His Word and by prayer, but one day, we'll see Him face to face!

> *"And someday I shall see Him face to face*
> *To thank and praise Him for His wondrous grace*
> *Which He gave to me when He made me free;*
> *The blessed Son of God called Jesus."*
> *"Jesus is the Sweetest Name I Know" Lela Long*

Won't it be wonderful to see the Lord Jesus face to face and spend eternity with Him in heaven!

Waah, Waah, Waah

"Then Moses heard the people weep throughout their families, every man in the door of his tent: and the anger of the LORD was kindled greatly; Moses also was displeased.

And Moses said unto the LORD, Wherefore hast thou afflicted thy servant? and wherefore have I not found favour in thy sight, that thou layest the burden of all this people upon me?

Have I conceived all this people? have I begotten them, that thou shouldest say unto me, Carry them in thy bosom, as a nursing father beareth the sucking child, unto the land which thou swarest unto their fathers?

Whence should I have flesh to give unto all this people? for they weep unto me, saying, Give us flesh, that we may eat.

I am not able to bear all this people alone, because it is too heavy for me.

And if thou deal thus with me, kill me, I pray thee, out of hand, if I have found favour in thy sight; and let me not see my wretchedness.

And the LORD said unto Moses, Gather unto me seventy men of the elders of Israel, whom thou knowest to be the elders of the people, and officers over them; and bring them unto the tabernacle of the congregation, that they may stand there with thee.

And I will come down and talk with thee there: and I will take of the spirit which is upon thee, and will put it upon them; and they shall bear the burden of the people

with thee, that thou bear it not thyself alone."
(Numbers 11:10-17)

As you can read, Moses was stressed out from the grief the Israelites gave him. They were complaining about the manna that God had provided. They said,

"We remember the fish, which we did eat in Egypt freely; the cucumbers, and the melons, and the leeks, and the onions, and the garlick:
But now our soul is dried away: there is nothing at all, beside this manna, before our eyes." (Numbers 11:5-6)

Did they really say that? Did they really talk about how nice it was in Egypt? Had they forgotten the cruel bondage? How Pharaoh had had their sons thrown into the river to drown or possibly be eaten by crocodiles? *"And Pharaoh charged all his people, saying, Every son that is born ye shall cast into the river, and every daughter ye shall save alive." (Exodus 1:22)*

Had they forgotten the plagues that God put on Egypt, sparing Israel? And how God destroyed Pharaoh and the mighty Egyptian army in the Red Sea? *"...and Israel saw the Egyptians dead upon the sea shore."* *(Exodus 14:30)*

Two lessons from the passage: first, don't whine. Most of us are tempted to whine at some point. As a cop, you may be tempted to whine about the job,

245

because things aren't perfect. They never are. But whining usually does no good, and if you've ever worked a tour of patrol duty with a whiny partner, you know how awful it is.

Whining is also a bad testimony for Christ. If you know Jesus as Saviour but you're tempted to whine, think instead of how the Lord brought you to Himself, and of things He's done for you. As the Johnson Oatman hymn, says to do, count your blessings:

> "Count your blessing, name them one by one;
> Count your blessings, see what God hath done;"

Second, when something's bothering you, pray and give God details. As *Psalm 62:8* says, *"...pour out your heart before him:"* Look how much detail Moses put into his prayer. God knew what Moses needed, but He met Moses' need when Moses prayed. Do you have problems you're trying to work out? Before you do anything else, pray and give God details and ask for help.

Treat Her Like a Lady

"Likewise, ye husbands, dwell with them according to knowledge, giving honour unto the wife,"
(1 Peter 3:7)

Jesus said, *"Have ye not read, that he which made them at the beginning made them male and female, And said, For this cause shall a man leave father and mother, and shall cleave to his wife: and they twain shall be one flesh?"* (Matthew 19:4-5)

When He said this, He pointed out three things: first, the truth of Scripture. He referenced *Genesis 2:24-* *"Therefore shall a man leave his father and his mother, and shall cleave unto his wife: and they shall be one flesh."* He also pointed out that we were created, not evolved: *"...he which made them at the beginning made them male and female,"*

Third, He pointed out that there's no such thing as same-sex marriage. Marriage is a sexual relationship—*"...they twain shall be one flesh"*—between a male and a female. Two people of the same gender may have a sexual relationship, but it's not a marriage. They may call it marriage, but it's not.

God ordained marriage, and He wants people to have happy marriages. He also gave us the info we need for a happy marriage. Law enforcement is notorious for a high divorce rate. You may be single and leery of marriage for that reason. Yes, the job puts stresses on marriage, but God's grace is still sufficient for even a police marriage to survive and thrive: *"My grace is sufficient for thee:" (2 Corinthians 12:9)*

The verse tells husbands to *"...dwell with them* [wives] *according to knowledge,"* A husband should know what his wife likes and dislikes, and act accordingly. That's not being henpecked. That's being a good husband.

You know your wife better now than when you first met her. You should know what pleases her and what doesn't. If you don't, take time to learn. Husbands should strive to please their wives. *1 Corinthians 7:33* says, *"But he that is married careth for the things that are of the world, how he may please his wife."*

Do things that please her. Do dishes. Or laundry. Or both. Give her flowers. Give her compliments. Give her a back massage. Give her your undivided attention. Treat her like you did when she was your girlfriend.

It also says, *"...giving honour unto the wife,"* Police wives do everything other wives do. They take care of kids and households. They also live with burdens that most other wives don't: toxic media, politics, crazy shifts, internal strife, and of course, danger. They deserve honor.

The guys and gals at work are not more important

than your wife. You may have heard it said that you spend more time with them than with her. It's true that all of you put your lives on the line for each other. But your people at work don't have you for better or worse until death do you part. They don't keep your home together or take care of your kids. Your wife does.

If you're a guy married to a policewoman, the same principles apply. She works in a difficult, often-dangerous, male-oriented world, since most cops and most criminals are men; but she's still a lady, so know what pleases her and treat her with honor.

Those are just two points from God's Word that will help you in your marriage if you'll do them. Being a good cop doesn't happen by accident. You need to work at it, but the result is worth the effort. A happy, thriving marriage won't happen by accident, either. You need to work at it, too. Yet the result is also well worth the effort. God tells us how to do that, and He always knows best.

Stay on God's Side

"And if it seem evil unto you to serve the LORD, choose you this day whom ye will serve; whether the gods which your fathers served that were on the other side of the flood, or the gods of the Amorites, in whose land ye dwell: but as for me and my house, we will serve the LORD." (Joshua 24:15)

Before the Revolutionary War, Patrick Henry gave a powerful speech that ended with, "...give me liberty, or give me death!" Nathan Hale, before he was hanged by the British as a spy, was reported to say, "I only regret that I have but one life to lose for my country."

Winston Churchill said that if England beat the Germans in World War II, then if the British Empire and Commonwealth lasted a thousand years, people would still say of England, "This was their finest hour."

Here may be Joshua's signature saying:

"...choose you this day whom ye will serve;...but as for me and my house, we will serve the LORD."

Joshua was Israel's second leader after Moses. Joshua was a soldier. He was brave. He knew what it meant to risk his life for Israel. After Israel left Egypt, a group of thugs led by one Amalek attacked Israel. They attacked the weakest of Israel's people. Joshua led the fight to defeat Amalek and his people.

Joshua was the leader who actually led the Israelites into the promised land. Once they arrived, they had to fight one battle after another against heathen peoples, almost none of whom wanted peace with Israel: *"There was not a city that made peace with the children of Israel, save the Hivites the inhabitants of Gibeon:"* *(Joshua 11:19)*

Most importantly, Joshua cared about pleasing God. During the time in the wilderness, he was one of twelve spies Moses sent to check out the land of Canaan. When the spies returned, Joshua and Caleb were the only ones who wanted to obey God and go into the land. The other ten convinced Israel that it couldn't be done, even though God had said He'd give them the victory.

As a result, God made Israel wander in the wilderness forty more years until all the rebels age twenty and older died. God even killed the spies who'd provoked Israel to disobey. In fact, He killed them first.

Once the Israelites entered Canaan, and after so many battles, *"...the land rested from war." (Joshua 11:23)* The land was divided between the tribes of Israel, and most--not all--of the heathen had been dealt with.

When Joshua warned Israel, *"...choose you this day whom ye will serve;"*, he was old and near death. He had a reason for this warning. Before Moses died, God told him, *"Behold, thou shalt sleep with thy fathers; and this people will rise up, and go a-whoring after the gods of the strangers of the land," (Deuteronomy 31:16)*

Israel's plunge into idolatry hadn't happened on Joshua's watch, but he knew it would happen eventually. God would chastise Israel as a nation for their sin. Yet individual people in Israel could still determine in their hearts to serve the Lord faithfully.

The warning to *"...choose you this day whom ye will serve...but as for me and my house, we will serve the LORD."* wasn't just for the nation, but for individuals in that nation to choose to serve the Lord. Even when Israel turned from God and suffered His chastisement, individual people in Israel still served Him faithfully.

The longer you're a cop, the more dysfunction, drama, petty politics, and who-knows-how-many other problems you'll see in your department. But you can still serve the Lord with your best work: *"Whether therefore ye eat, or drink, or whatsoever ye do, do all to the glory of God." (1 Corinthians 10:31)*

Even in church, unfortunately, you may meet people who don't really care about serving Christ. Strive to serve Him, anyway. Take the attitude Joshua had: *"...choose you this day whom ye will serve;...but as for me and my house, we will serve the LORD."*

Striking Fear in Evildoers' Hearts

"Let every soul be subject unto the higher powers. For there is no power but of God: the powers that be are ordained of God. Whosoever therefore resisteth the power, resisteth the ordinance of God: and they that resist shall receive to themselves damnation. For rulers are not a terror to good works, but to the evil. Wilt thou then not be afraid of the power? do that which is good, and thou shalt have praise of the same: For he is the minister of God to thee for good. But if thou do that which is evil, be afraid; for he beareth not the sword in vain: for he is the minister of God, a revenger to execute wrath upon him that doeth evil."
(Romans 13:1-4)

This passage is about police. The terms *"higher powers"* and *"powers that be"* refer to government. The phrase, "the powers that be" came from the Bible. Criminals are people who "resist the power" and "resist the ordinance of God". Cops are on the job, to be *"not a terror to good works, but to the evil."*

"EVIL" is the word God uses to describe what criminals do. E-V-I-L. Burglars do evil. Robbers, rapists, drug dealers, and thieves do evil. The "ruler" in this passage, also called the *"minister of God",* is the police. He or she is not a ruler in the sense of a monarch but an agent of the government, acting on behalf of citizens. He or she is the one God has appointed to deal with those who do evil.

The Bible tells us that criminals should fear the police: *"But if thou* [criminal] *do that which is evil, be afraid; for he* [police] *beareth not the sword in vain:"* The police officer is *"...the minister of God, a revenger to execute wrath upon him that doeth evil."*

Cops are God's ministers to punish evildoers and put fear into their hearts. The warning, *"...he beareth not the sword in vain:"* is God's authorization for use of force, whether the officer's "sword" be physical force, a Taser, baton, or firearm.

Criminals have used deadly weapons ever since Cain murdered Abel. God's Word talks of police having deadly weapons to meet evildoers on their own terms.

Johnny may have no moral qualms about sticking a gun in the clerk's face at the mom-and-pop store, but he may think twice if he's afraid the cops will pull up and shoot him while his gun is in his hand—or his BB gun with the orange tip removed to make it look real. Fear of the police may be the only thing that keeps Johnny from committing crime, but if it works, that's a good thing. That's Bible.

But if criminals have no fear factor, no "terror to the evil" to hold them in check, they'll commit crime and terrorize innocent citizens. When cops are micromanaged for rule violations and their money is taken away by suspensions, they learn to be afraid: not of criminals but their own department.

As a result, they learn not to be proactive and risk a suspension by some rule violation. Criminals have no fear, they take full advantage, and decent citizens in tough neighborhoods, who can't afford to move out, suffer the most.

Cops should do their jobs with integrity, but leaders should also remember why cops are out there to begin with. They should also remember that police work is a morale-driven job. You can force an officer to comply with regulations, but you can't force him to be enthusiastic.

You may have heard it said, "The floggings will continue until morale improves." When leaders *"...strain at a gnat, and swallow a camel." (Matthew 23:24)* by too much attention to rules and not enough attention to police work, they can destroy the motivation of hard-working officers and end up hurting decent citizens and helping the very evildoers whom God's Word says should be afraid.

Please, Don't Eat Your Gun

"And when they had laid many stripes upon them [Paul and Silas], *they cast them into prison, charging the jailer to keep them safely:*

Who, having received such a charge, thrust them into the inner prison, and made their feet fast in the stocks.

And at midnight Paul and Silas prayed, and sang praises unto God: and the prisoners heard them.

And suddenly there was a great earthquake, so that the foundations of the prison were shaken: and immediately all the doors were opened, and every one's bands were loosed.

And the keeper of the prison awaking out of his sleep, and seeing the prison doors open, he drew out his sword, and would have killed himself, supposing that the prisoners had been fled.

But Paul cried with a loud voice, saying, Do thyself no harm: for we are all here.

Then he called for a light, and sprang in, and came trembling, and fell down before Paul and Silas,

And brought them out, and said, Sirs, what must I do to be saved?

And they said, Believe on the Lord Jesus Christ, and thou shalt be saved, and thy house.

And they spake unto him the word of the Lord, and to all that were in his house.

And he took them the same hour of the night, and washed their stripes; and was baptized, he and all his, straightway.

And when he had brought them into his house, he set

meat before them, and rejoiced, believing in God with all his house." (Acts 16:23-34)

Paul and Silas were thrown into jail. How could they pray and sing in jail? Because the Lord Jesus had said,

"Blessed are ye, when men shall revile you, and persecute you, and shall say all manner of evil against you falsely, for my sake.
Rejoice, and be exceeding glad: for great is your reward in heaven: for so persecuted they the prophets which were before you." (Matthew 5:11-12)

The jailer dozed off. Ever doze off on a hospital prisoner detail? What if you dozed off and your prisoner escaped? No doubt you'd be in trouble, but not so much trouble as this jailer was.

Two commentaries describe what happened to a guard who let a prisoner escape. *Albert Barnes' Notes on the New Testament* says he had to suffer their punishment. *Family Bible Notes* says the punishment was death.

Either way, when he awoke and thought the prisoners had fled, what do you think was going through his mind? As far as he was concerned, he was in a bad situation with only one way out: suicide.

Why do cops kill themselves? Why does anyone kill himself? I was a cop thirty-three years, but I'm not

257

arrogant enough to think I have all the answers. Maybe a personal or job-related problem. Maybe a problem the person created for himself. Maybe the person's heart has been insidiously poisoned over time from all the junk cops deal with on the job. Maybe people come to the point where they think there's no hope.

Well, here's hope! Paul saw what the jailer was about to do and yelled that they were all there. The light of hope breaking through the darkness of despair! None of the prisoners tried to escape, even with their shackles loosed!

The jailer knew he needed Christ. Paul and Silas told him how to be saved, and instead of making the worst decision in the world—suicide, he made the best, most joyful decision in the world: to receive the Lord Jesus by faith as his personal Saviour.

Suicide may seem the only answer in a crisis, but it leaves behind broken hearts, unanswered questions, and guilty feelings. Like the jailer, someone on the verge of suicide may see no other way out.

Yet there is hope! God is the God of hope! *"Now the God of hope fill you with all joy and peace in believing,"* *(Romans 15:13)* God's love and grace through Christ can steer people from self-destruction, and turn grief to joy, *"...mourning into dancing:"* *(Psalm 30:11)*

Fellowship with the King

"For thus saith the high and lofty One that inhabiteth eternity, whose name is Holy; I dwell in the high and holy place, with him also that is of a contrite and humble spirit, to revive the spirit of the humble, and to revive the heart of the contrite ones." (Isaiah 57:15)

Ever hear people call God "the man upstairs"? Flippant terms like that show a lack of knowledge and a lack of reverence for God. When Isaiah the prophet saw God in His glory, He was a fearsome sight:

"In the year that king Uzziah died I saw also the Lord sitting upon a throne, high and lifted up, and his train filled the temple. Above it stood the seraphims: each one had six wings; with twain he covered his face, and with twain he covered his feet, and with twain he did fly. And one cried unto another, and said, Holy, holy, holy, is the LORD of hosts: the whole earth is full of his glory. And the posts of the door moved at the voice of him that cried, and the house was filled with smoke." (Isaiah 6:1-4)

Imagine God on His throne, flanked by seraphims-- angels. The Bible says angels are *"greater in power and might" (2 Peter 2:11)* than people, and fearsome looking. Scripture makes this clear. When Gabriel went to Zacharias and told him he'd be father to John the Baptist, his first words were, *"Fear not, Zacharias:" (Luke 1:13)* When he appeared to tell Mary she'd be

Jesus' mother, he said, *"Fear not, Mary:" (Luke 1:30)*

When the angel appeared to the shepherds to announce Jesus' birth, his first words were, *"Fear not:" (Luke 2:10)* How powerful and fearsome they must be! How infinitely more powerful and fearsome God must be!

When the prophet Isaiah saw God in His majesty, he realized how sinful he himself was: *"Then said I, Woe is me! for I am undone; because I am a man of unclean lips, and I dwell in the midst of a people of unclean lips: for mine eyes have seen the King, the LORD of hosts." (Isaiah 6:5)*

When we realize how holy and mighty God is, we also see how sinful and unworthy we are, like Isaiah. Yet as our verse says, God also dwells *"...with him also that is of a contrite and humble spirit,"* Psalm 34:18 also says, *"The LORD is nigh unto them that are of a broken heart; and saveth such as be of a contrite spirit."* That's what Jesus' death was about: God in His holiness reaching down to man in his sinfulness.

God not only wants us to have forgiveness of sins and be saved. He also wants to give us encouragement for daily life. God gave us His Word for encouragement and strength by reading it and letting Him speak to our hearts through it.

As a cop, unfortunately, you can find discouragement

in many sources, some from within your own department or local government. One training officer told me long ago that I'd get more stress from inside the department than outside.

The place for strength and encouragement is God's sanctuary. *Psalm 96:6* says, *"Honour and majesty are before him: strength and beauty are in his sanctuary."* You may think of church when you hear the word "sanctuary." That's true. If you can go to a service at a Bible-preaching church, don't skip it.

But even outside church hours, your sanctuary--the place where God gives you strength and beauty--can be any quiet place that you open His Word and He speaks to your heart, and you talk to Him in thanksgiving and prayer. It can even be your patrol car when you have down time. God wants fellowship with you. That's a big reason we have His Word.

The Main Thing

"Looking unto Jesus the author and finisher of our faith;" (Hebrews 12:2)

When you're a cop, it's easy to get your focus off "the main thing." You may see officers and bosses who don't care about the job. You may see a hierarchy willing to throw cops under the bus over a "controversial" incident, regardless of who was right. You may see cops disciplined for excellent police work that wasn't picture perfect. And how exactly does one do perfect police work?

Some may say the job has changed. No, it hasn't. People in power may set bad policies that make life easier for themselves--and criminals--and harder for decent people, and the social/political environments may be more criminal-friendly, but the job hasn't changed.

Criminals are still the predators that they've always been. They take advantage when cops are handcuffed and they terrorize innocent citizens, often who are smaller, weaker, and defenseless. Decent people still need cops who are willing to put their lives on the line to help them.

On a "male with a gun" or "store being robbed" call, someone has to do the dirty work: hit the lights and siren, snake through traffic, and face off against a dangerous suspect who may be armed, younger, bigger, stronger, and/or on drugs, and not weighed down with equipment.

Someone has to go to the dangerous place, *"the valley of the shadow of death" (Psalm 23:4)* where he or she could be dead in the next moment. That hasn't changed.

People who don't do police work, and who don't talk with crime victims, may have no clue about what's involved. That's a shame, and you can't control what other people do, but you can do your personal best to help decent people.

You know them. They may quietly point a "he went that way" finger when you're chasing a suspect, or mouth a "thank you" as you're hauling away a prisoner. They don't want to be on camera for the criminals to see them, but they appreciate you. Keep your focus.

You may meet twenty people on your tour. Most of them may greet you or at least be polite, but one may spit in your direction. Which of those twenty do you think you'll remember best? Probably the spitter.

Don't let people like that steer your focus. Troublemakers may try to get more attention but keep your focus on the decent people. The main thing in police work is helping decent people by confronting criminals.

Likewise, the main thing for a Christian is to serve the Lord and live to please Him and tell others how to receive Him as Saviour, just like someone told you. So keep your focus on *"...Jesus the author and finisher of our faith;"*

God's Power Source

"Let the word of Christ dwell in you richly in all wisdom;" (Colossians 3:16)

As a cop, you know it's important to commit info to memory. If you write tickets, you probably have the codes for speeding and stop sign violation memorized. If you make crime reports, you probably know the codes for burglary, breaking and entering, auto theft, and domestic violence by heart.

If you have time on the job, you can probably give a suspect his Miranda rights by memory. If he's a frequent flyer, he can probably give them to you the same way. You may also make a habit of memorizing license plates for cars that are stolen or wanted.

Seeing a hot license plate rolling on the street is also an adrenaline junkie's dream, especially a vanity plate. A stolen vanity plate is like a neon sign on a car, especially when the boss had just said at roll call that it's hot.

The more you know the job by heart, the better you are at it, and the more you enjoy it. If you know Jesus as Saviour, Bible memorizing will also help you in your Christian life. When you first heard about trusting Jesus as Saviour, you may not have known it but God was using *"...the voice of his word." (Psalm 103:20)* to convince you of your need for Christ.

It wasn't great salesmanship by some Christian. It was because God dealt with your heart: *"God is faithful, by whom ye were called* [boldface added] *unto the fellowship of his Son Jesus Christ our Lord." (1 Corinthians 1:9)* God called you. Whoever witnessed to you was just the human instrument God used.

Once you know Jesus as Saviour, though, God still has many things to tell you through His Word. God has many things He wants to say, if we're willing to listen: *"...when thou awakest, it shall talk with thee." (Proverbs 6:22)*

You *"Let the word of Christ dwell in you richly in all wisdom;"* by reading and memorizing passages that speak to your heart. The more you do this, the more God speaks to your heart, and the more you enjoy your Christian life.

Jesus said, *"These things* [God's words] *have I spoken unto you, that my joy might remain in you, and that your joy might be full." (John 15:11)* Are you saved but maybe don't enjoy your Christian life? When did you last sit down and open God's Word? You may be busy, but this is important. There's always time for what's important.

As you memorize Scriptures, you'll find many passages to help you on the job. We've already seen from the Bible that God ordained police work. If God ordained it, then, He would have provided us wisdom

266

on how to deal with the job and its problems. And He provided plenty.

You'll find many short but helpful thoughts in God's Word. For instance, God's Word will help you resist temptation: *"Thy word have I hid in mine heart, that I might not sin against thee." (Psalm 119:11)* Ephesians *4:29* will help you watch your words: *"Let no corrupt communication proceed out of your mouth,"* Psalm *18:39* is great on a dangerous call: *"For thou hast girded me with strength unto the battle:"*

Need to make a judgment call? *James 1:5* tells us to pray: *"If any of you lack wisdom, let him ask of God,"* Things aren't always black-and-white on this job. If you're ever in a gray area, what do you do? You call a boss or a more experienced officer to help you decide.

Well, think of prayer as calling on someone who's more experienced to help you. Who knows more about police work, or everything else, for that matter, than God? *Psalm 147:5* says, *"...his understanding is infinite."*

Keep a small Bible with you at work. If you have a little dead time, open it up instead of the newspaper or some magazine and let God speak to your heart. The Bible is literally a bottomless well of encouragement, challenge, comfort, instruction, and grace.

Make the Best of It

"Thus saith the LORD of hosts, the God of Israel, unto all that are carried away captives, whom I have caused to be carried away from Jerusalem unto Babylon; Build ye houses, and dwell in them; and plant gardens, and eat the fruit of them; Take ye wives, and beget sons and daughters; and take wives for your sons, and give your daughters to husbands, that they may bear sons and daughters; that ye may be increased there, and not diminished. And seek the peace of the city whither I have caused you to be carried away captives, and pray unto the LORD for it: for in the peace thereof shall ye have peace." (Jeremiah 29:4-7)

Judah had turned their backs on the true God and worshipped false gods. Sin had immersed their culture. God let the Babylonians take them into captivity.

God didn't suddenly love the Babylonians better, but God used the Babylonians, as ungodly as they were, to chasten Judah for their sin.

Many Jews went into captivity who weren't guilty, such as Daniel the prophet and his three friends. That's one thing sin does: it hurts innocent people. As a cop, you see all the time how people's sin hurts others around them.

Alcohol is a great example of a sin that hurts innocent people, in terms of motorists killed and maimed, families ruined, spouses abused (how many times have you heard an abuse victim say, "he's a great guy, except when he's drunk"?) kids neglected, wages lost, and employee absences. If you drink alcohol—even if you don't have any of these problems--you support the liquor industry which contributes to them.

Back to our Scripture: these words were apparently written to people who wanted to serve the true God. No doubt they were heartbroken over what was going on. God told them to build houses, plant gardens, find spouses (among the Jews, not the idol-worshipping Babylonians) for themselves and their kids, and basically make the best of things. A few verses later, God gave them these words of encouragement:

"For I know the thoughts that I think toward you, saith the LORD, thoughts of peace, and not of evil, to give you an expected end. Then shall ye call upon me, and ye shall go and pray unto me, and I will hearken unto you. And ye shall seek me, and find me, when ye shall search for me with all your heart." (Jeremiah 29:11-13)

God was chastening His people, but He hadn't forgotten or forsaken them. He wanted to do them good and give them peace. He told them to seek Him with all their heart, and even in Babylon, they could walk by faith in Him and make the best of their situation.

If you're a cop, you may not like how things are going

where you work. You may want to go to another unit or another department. But if you know Jesus as Saviour, God has you where you are for a reason.

So, instead of wishing you were in SWAT or Narcotics (and by the way, how do you know that the officers in SWAT or Narcotics are all that happy?), ask the Lord to help you make the best of where you are now. Put in for a transfer if you want, but also learn to be content if you don't get it.

Your workplace needs good cops. Most importantly, your workplace needs cops who care about people and are willing to share Christ's love. Ask the Lord to help you to be a good officer, and a good witness to others for Jesus.

Built on the Solid Rock

"...upon this rock I will build my church; and the gates of hell shall not prevail against it."
(Matthew 16:18)

Church is important. We know it's important because the Lord Jesus said it's important. He referred to church as *"my church"* (boldface added). It's Jesus' church, as the passage says. Church is mentioned many times in the Bible. It's an institution God ordained, not an idea someone just thought up.

A church is like a police department, in a way. If you're a cop, you work for a law enforcement agency somewhere, like a city police department or county sheriff's office. What if a guy told you he was a cop. Of course, you'll ask where. What if he said, "I don't work for any department. I just work around." You wouldn't believe for one minute that he was a cop! There's no such thing as a freelance police officer.

In the same way, don't try to be a freelance Christian. If you're saved, you need to be in a church where God's Word is preached and where you serve the Lord.

Some may say you don't have to go to a church to be a Christian. Technically that's true. If you've received Jesus as your personal Saviour, that makes you a Christian. *Galatians 3:26* says, *"For ye are all the children of God by faith in Christ Jesus."*

271

It's also true, however, that once you receive Jesus as Saviour, you are no longer your own. You belong to Him, and it's for you to glorify Him in your life: *"For ye are bought with a price: therefore glorify God in your body, and in your spirit, which are God's." (1 Corinthians 6:20)*

Being a Christian and being a *useful* Christian are two different things. To illustrate the point, I'm a licensed practical nurse. Really. I have a valid license to practice nursing in Ohio. However, I haven't practiced nursing in a long time, so I can't just walk into a facility and go to work. I'd need training and guidance to be a *useful* nurse.

If you want to be an *obedient* and *useful* Christian, you need to be faithful in a Bible-preaching, soul-winning church. If you want to be a *strong* Christian, you also need to be faithful to church.

Church is a place for a Christian to gain strength. *"...strength and beauty are in his sanctuary." (Psalm 96:6)* All the sin you deal with on the job and your daily life can sap your spiritual strength. Make it a point to attend church faithfully. Faithful attendance in God's sanctuary will help you to be a strong Christian.

Church is also important because it is God's chosen operating base for spreading the gospel. The church is in a battle with *"the gates of hell."* The purpose of a church—that is, the people in it--is to tell others how

Jesus died for their sins, was buried, and rose again; and by coming to Him in repentance and faith and receiving Him as their personal Saviour, they will have forgiveness of sins and eternal life in heaven.

On the other hand, the fallen angel known as Satan doesn't want people to be saved. He wants people to die in their sins and spend eternity in hell with him: *"Those by the way side are they that hear; then cometh the devil, and taketh away the word out of their hearts, lest they should believe and be saved." (Luke 8:12)*

He also wants to ruin saved people so they won't be effective for Christ. Peter warned believers, *"Be sober, be vigilant; because your adversary the devil, as a roaring lion, walketh about, seeking whom he may devour:" (1 Peter 5:8)*

A church is like a police department in another way: a department may be transparent, accountable, avoid "implicit bias", and all the other politically correct terms; but if laws aren't enforced and criminals aren't dealt with, the police department isn't doing its job.

A church also may claim to be loving and welcoming, but if people don't hear how to be saved and hear truth from God's Word, the church isn't doing its job, either.

If you're saved, please find a Bible-believing, soul-winning church to attend faithfully where you can be encouraged and challenged in your Christian life.

Say it With Balloons

"A man's gift maketh room for him," (Proverbs 18:16)

When you give someone a gift, even a small one, you make a good impression. If you're a guy and you open a door for a lady, she appreciates the courtesy. I've opened doors for ladies many times. Not once did a lady object.

For cops, giving gifts is good public relations. Try to do PR work when you can. Even in tough areas, most people want the police to deal with criminals aggressively. They may be leery of police, though, because of stories they've heard, and they may have heard only one side—the suspect's side—of the story.

You should be proactive and aggressive against criminals, but the more proactive you are, the more you're in the public eye. People watch you work. They may not know you by name, but they remember your face AND HOW YOU ACT TOWARD PEOPLE.

Our church had a function at a rec center in the area where I used to work. I was in a suit and approached some young guys near the basketball court. I invited them to church. One of them said, "You used to work 4th District." I had. He remembered me over 2 ½ years after I'd left.

When you do PR work, you show your human side and promote yourself and your department. Criminals don't do that because they aren't good guys. They're called bad guys for a reason. They don't help people and give to them. They hurt people and take from them.

PR work can also make the job fun. One evening as I was on a ride-along as a chaplain, we went to a domestic call. The four-year old son of one of the combatants was also on scene. I saw that the problem was little more than an argument, so I pulled out my balloons and made a sword. I asked his mom if he could have it. She said yes.

I gave it to him and made myself one, too. The officers handled the call while the boy and I had a sword fight. He enjoyed the attention, and I believe we left a good impression of the police on the boy's mind and his mom's.

When I was a patrol boss, we had a call of two young boys who'd been sexually molested by their father. I still recall the devastation on one boy's face. I wasn't very good with balloons at the time, but I figured if I could brighten their day a little, it was worth a try.

Balloons are my favorite PR tool. They're widely available and you can find instructions on the internet for many different balloon figures. Girls usually like flower rings, and swords are usually a hit with boys. Both are easy to make, and if you can't inflate them by mouth, you can keep a small pump handy.

You may have some talent you can use for PR. One buddy of mine did magic. Don't be afraid to put some talent to use, especially if you involve kids. Kids love attention, and they often don't get enough of it.

Even if you don't think you're talented, you can give people time—even a minute or so. When you get coffee at the gas station, greet other customers. Ask how they're doing, what they think of the local sports team, anything for the sake of a brief but friendly conversation.

If kids are playing ball, watch the game a little. If they're collecting money for a community sports program, shell out a buck or two. Don't be a cheapskate.

You may have heard debate about whether cops should be warriors or guardians. Cops actually need to be both: warriors ready to battle against criminals, but guardians for citizens, looking out for their well-being. Showing your human side as a guardian to citizens helps them have confidence in you.

If you know Jesus as Saviour, add one more moniker: missionary. When you engage people in a personal way, you never know when the Lord will open a door for you to share Christ, even in a small way.

Antidote for Heart-Poisoning

"Mine eye affecteth mine heart because of all the daughters of my city." (Lamentations 3:51)

In Lamentations, Jeremiah tells how God's people were taken captive because of chronic sin. Maybe he wrote these words because he was heartbroken at seeing the young ladies, the *"daughters of my city"*, taken as captives because of their parents' sins. At any rate, Jeremiah's heart was affected by what he saw. That's an important truth, *"Mine eye affecteth mine heart..."*

Proverbs 4:23 says, *"Keep thy heart with all diligence; for out of it are the issues of life."* God tells us plainly to keep our hearts, so it must be possible to keep our hearts from becoming cold and indifferent about God. God wouldn't give us a command that He knew we couldn't keep. *Proverbs 23:7* also says, *"For as he thinketh in his heart, so is he:"* To put it another way, "As a man thinks in his heart, so is he."

You can be tempted as a cop to be mean, cold-hearted, bitter, and uncaring, but you don't have to be. You can love the Lord and care about people as a cop, if you want. As you decide you'll be, so you'll be. If you know Jesus as Saviour, He's promised grace to help you have a right heart toward Him. *Philippians 4:13* says, *"I can do all things through Christ which strengtheneth me."*

Here's where *"Mine eye affecteth mine heart..."* comes in. It says that what we see affects how we think in our hearts. As a cop, you see a lot of things that affect your heart: things like domestic fights with live-in lovers in roach-infested apartments; bloody, gory death scenes; and sex offenders who do vile things to kids.

Things you see on the job do affect your heart, and you often can't control dealing with them. But what about things you *can* control? Do you watch TV shows or movies with sex, vulgar words, or violence? Or listen to music with foul lyrics?

Would you let your younger kids watch or listen? If you wouldn't, why not? Would these things have a bad effect on them? What about how they affect *you?* You may say they don't affect you, but God's word says they do: The *"Mine eye affecteth mine heart..."* principle applies to adults as well as kids.

Psalm 101:3 says, *"I will set no wicked thing before mine eyes:"* You don't choose the runs you're called to, but you choose your entertainment. Any show, even a "cop show" or "cop movie" where sin is glorified and exploited, is wicked.

Hollywood isn't about morals, and don't expect Hollywood to support cops. Hollywood is about money. When you put wicked things in front of your eyes, they'll affect your heart in a bad way.

278

Moreover, if you spend little time in God's Word, and you don't go regularly to a church where God's Word is preached faithfully, you're not getting much good food through your "eye-gate" or "ear-gate." If your heart food consists largely of what you see on the job, how you entertain yourself, and very little of God's Word, your heart is likely to become cold toward God.

You may know officers who are saved but they're indifferent about God. They may even know in their hearts that things aren't right, but they're still cold. You may feel that way yourself at times. Well, here's good news. Nobody has to become that way, and even people who have become that way don't have to stay that way.

Our verse says, *"Mine eye affecteth mine heart..."*, and that principle works both ways. If you can affect your heart in an evil way by feeding it garbage, you can also affect it in a good way by feeding it with God's Word, God's music, and faithful preaching.

If you're saved but you've neglected God's Word and God's church, then do what the Lord told the Christians at Laodicea to do: *"...be zealous therefore, and repent." (Revelation 3:19)* Ask the Lord to forgive you your neglect and help you feed regularly on His truth.

Last Day on the Street

"Yet forty days, and Nineveh shall be overthrown."
(Jonah 3:4)

Here's the Cliff notes version of the story of Jonah:
God told Jonah to go to Nineveh to warn them to repent
or else. Instead, Jonah boarded a ship headed for
Tarshish to flee from the Lord. God sent a storm which
threw the ship around wildly.

Jonah knew God had sent the storm because of him
and asked the sailors to throw him overboard, and the
sea would be calm. They didn't want to do that but
eventually they did, asking God to forgive them. God
then commanded a whale to swallow Jonah. Unlike
Jonah, the whale obeyed God.

Eventually the whale vomited up Jonah on dry land
at Nineveh. Jonah went into the city and said, *"Yet forty
days, and Nineveh shall be overthrown."* He may have
said other things, but the Scripture only records these
eight words.

When the king heard this warning, he stepped off his
throne and clothed himself in sackcloth and ashes, to
signify repentance for sin. He also commanded all the
citizens of the city to do the same. God saw their
repentance, and He did not destroy the city.

Were those eight words of Jonah the first time the

Ninevites heard of the true God and His call to repentance? Or had God been dealing with their hearts in some way for a while, and Jonah's words were the straw that broke the camel's back?

Quite possibly, they had known of the true God and His holiness and calls for repentance in the past. In *1 Corinthians 3:6*, Paul says, *"I have planted, Apollos watered; but God gave the increase."* So, it seems likely that Jonah's message was not the first they'd heard.

Here's a helpful point: when you mention the Lord to people, you don't know how God has already been dealing with their hearts, so even a few words can be helpful. Don't be afraid to share even a few words with people if the Lord opens a door.

My last day on patrol was September 2, 2014. I started the shift at 8:00 am. Not long after the start of the shift, one of the crews called me to a house to take photos for a domestic violence case. I took the photos and returned to the station to download them.

I also conferred with another patrol crew that was training rookies. About 9:00 am the dispatcher called for a car to go to the abortion clinic. The abortion clinic called every so often about protesters. I planned to go there myself; not that I had any love for the abortion clinic, but bosses were supposed to go when the abortion clinic called, and I had to do my job.

Shortly after the abortion clinic call, the dispatcher broadcast a call of a male shooting on East 140 between Kinsman and Milverton. I was still at the station. When I heard that call, I bailed out the door and jumped into my patrol car. So much for the abortion clinic.

I pulled out onto Kinsman Road, the main thoroughfare running through the middle of the 4th District. I hit the red-and-blues and weaved east through traffic toward East 140. As I did, I thought uneasily about how a lot of rookies were working that morning. Everyone gets a baptism of fire sooner or later, but I'd rather they get their feet wet a little in patrol. Other cars were enroute as well.

I reached East 140 and turned left. I didn't see or hear anything out of the ordinary: no screaming, no bodies in the street, no blood, nothing. I rolled a short distance north. I saw two men off to my left and pulled left to the curb to find out if they had seen or heard anything.

Just as I pulled to the curb, I saw a man outside my driver's window, maybe ten feet away. He was holding a revolver, pointing it at me and yelling, "What's up? What's up?" He had the drop on me, no doubt about it.

I don't recall yelling at him to drop the gun. I don't recall that I had time. I snatched my 9mm from its holster, pointed it out the window, and fired. He was still standing. I fired again. I was sure I was too close to miss, but he was still standing. I fired again.

I pulled away, drove around a parked car, and stopped. I threw my car into park, exited, and walked back to him. From the time I first saw him to my last shot was maybe five seconds.

I hadn't missed. He lay on the tree lawn, his gun in his hand. He stared dully, his eyes partly open. An ugly dark red blotch spread across the lower front of his white t-shirt. The cylinder had also popped out of his revolver, so I knew he was no longer a threat.

I called on the radio for Emergency Medical Services and the shooting team. Cars started showing up. People stood all around, watching. I told the responding officers to grab the people standing around and get their names and their stories.

Then I realized that he may still be alive. We had learned early on the job that until a doctor pronounces someone dead, we should treat him like he's alive. I put on latex gloves and started CPR. I didn't know if I was doing any good pumping his chest, but I had to try.

I don't recall being mad at him for trying to kill me. It was by God's grace that I wasn't. At that point, he looked so pathetic lying there. I was just trying to save his life. I also bent over him and said, "You need to accept Jesus as your Saviour."

I obviously didn't give him a good gospel presentation, but I didn't have time to pull out my New

Testament (doesn't everyone carry a New Testament on duty?) and share Scripture with him. Anything I said would have to be fast, because his remaining life span was obviously down to minutes, if not seconds.

EMS took him to the hospital. I learned later that he'd died. I wasn't surprised. Grieved, yes. But not surprised.

My boss, Lieutenant Tim Gaertner, ordered the scene taped off. Several members of the Command Staff showed up, as well as Homicide, Internal Affairs, the Crime Scene Unit, the Coroner, and of course the media.

This wasn't my first rodeo, as a buddy of mine had said, so I didn't feel overly emotional; just a heavy-hearted "here we go again" feeling." I knew the drill and how things would go.

I called Debbie and told her the bad news that I had just shot a guy and he didn't look good. Our teenage children had also found out. A local activist group, Peace Alliance, also showed up, hoping to keep the citizens calm.

Last Day on the Street—Epilog

Lt. Ron Timm, the Homicide boss, asked me on the scene how many times I'd fired.

"Three," I said without hesitation.

"Are you sure?" he asked. I caught skepticism on his face. "Count your rounds." I pulled out my magazine and counted.

Six rounds were missing.

"Why are you missing six rounds?" he asked.

I was stumped. I was sure I had only fired three. The only explanation I could think of was that my son and I had gone shooting about a month and a half ago. Yet even that didn't make sense. Lt. Timm didn't comment further.

Lt. Gaertner encouraged me as he assisted me off the scene. He also told me kindly that this would be my last day on the street. I'd known and respected him for years as a cop and as a boss, but I was sure that the investigation would be quick because the shooting itself was so cut-and-dried. Yet he was right.

Homicide seized my handgun, which is standard practice, and arranged for me to have another. That was a bummer, since I'd bought that handgun and now I'd have to wait seven years to get it back, since it must be held as possible evidence in the event of a civil lawsuit.

The initial investigation took hours to complete. I also had to go to the hospital for a blood exposure treatment because I'd gotten the suspect's blood on my hand. I didn't arrive home until about 9:00 pm.

Over the next few days or so, I received countless text messages, phone calls, and emails asking if I were ok and people saying they were thinking about me and praying for me. Those words of encouragement meant so much.

Unfortunately, I was now on restricted duty. That meant no street duty, no part-time, and no extra money. Bad news, especially around Christmas. Truth to tell, I wasn't praising the Lord and quoting *Romans 8:28*, saying how *"...all things work together for good to them that love God,"* In fact, I was a bit of a grouch.

The Ferguson, Missouri shooting had also occurred less than a month earlier, so the national anti-police media hurricane was already gathering steam.

About a week after the shooting, I went to Homicide with Lieutenant Brian Betley and Sergeant Jerry Zarlenga from the FOP to make my official statement. Lt. Timm played a 911 recording of a lady who had called the morning of the shooting.

We listened to the recording of her talking with the clerk. As she talked, we heard five or six shots in the background from the same caliber handgun. Those were my shots. Obviously, I'd fired six, which explained why six rounds were missing.

I hadn't lied when Lt. Timm asked, and he knew that. I just didn't remember firing that many times. Perceptual distortions aren't uncommon for officers in shootings.

After the shooting, I was detailed to the police gym at headquarters for a time. Standard practice again. Most people who worked there knew me and knew what had happened. They'd ask if I were ok and express their concern, which I appreciated.

Mike Morales, a sergeant in the Inspection Unit, was a great encouragement. Sort of. He saw me in the hall and asked, "Haven't you been indicted yet?"

Thanks, Mike. I love you, too.

Cop humor, you know.

I had also gone to the County Prosecutor's Office a couple of times to see how the case was progressing. The prosecutor became understandably irritated and explained patiently that since I was technically the "suspect," my being at the Prosecutor's Office had an appearance of impropriety. As a result, he said he may have to appoint a special prosecutor and then I'd *really* see a delay. I got the hint. I didn't go back.

Seven-and-a-half months later, I was called into the office of County Prosecutor Timothy McGinty. One of the first things he said was, "God was with you that morning."

He told me they'd found two live rounds for the suspect's gun. Each round had five firing strikes, total of ten misfires. He'd fired at one guy, then was going around pointing his gun at people and saying, "Who's next?"

I can't say how many of those were aimed at me or at the neighbors. Yet Prosecutor McGinty told Police Chief Calvin Williams in a letter that neutral witnesses were adamant that the suspect *"...was firing at the police officer as he pulled up in his marked zone car."*

After I was cleared, Debbie said she didn't want me to go back to patrol. I wanted to go back, but the shooting and its aftermath—publicity, inquiring friends, lengthy investigation, financial hardship, kids' fear of retaliation, grouchy husband, etc.--had been an ordeal for her, too.

I didn't want to disrespect her and damage our marriage for the sake of four more months in patrol, so I stayed in the Record File Section.

Prosecutor McGinty was right about God blessing that day. In addition to the misfires, we had basically no negative community reaction. Unlike Ferguson, we had no protests, no "hands up don't shoot," and relatively little media attention. A crowd had gathered, which is to be expected, but there was little or no trouble.

In fact, one officer working patrol that day told me a guy in the neighborhood walked up to the patrol car and asked him if I were okay. Think about that for a minute. Just after a fatal police shooting involving a white cop and a black suspect, he didn't ask about the guy I'd shot. He asked about me. That was touching.

It's also important to note that East 140-Kinsman is a high-crime area. Supporting the police can be risky, but people were honest and cooperative. Every statement I read in the report backed me up. I wanted to send the witnesses a card or other expression of gratitude, but one Homicide detective didn't like the idea in case one of the local predators intercepted the mail.

I'd worked patrol in high-crime neighborhoods most of my career and loved it. It was what I'd come onto the job to do. I can't speak for other cities, but I can speak for Cleveland. I've worked long enough in high-crime, inner-city neighborhoods, including black neighborhoods, to know that many decent people live in these areas. They are desperately scared of violent criminals and want police to do their jobs aggressively.

I can't say how many times people in these areas have quietly had our backs.

After another shooting incident several years back, I was at my patrol car as the post-shooting investigation started. An older lady came out of her house onto her front porch and wanted to know what had happened. Quite a few shots had been fired. I'm sure she'd heard the gunfire.

I told her we'd had a problem but it had been resolved. How's that for a vague answer? It seemed to satisfy her, though, and she turned to go back into the house. Before she did, she turned back to me and said, "Thank you."

People like that lady are the ones cops in the inner city put their lives on the line for every day. They're also the ones who suffer most when people in power set restrictive policies that make it hard for cops to help them and easier for criminals to hurt them, which frustrates me to no end.

If you work in a high-crime area, you may be the only defense decent people have. Pursue criminals as aggressively as you can, but have compassion for people, as well. Know when to be a warrior and when to be a guardian.

Someone Has to Do It

"Go ye into all the world, and preach the gospel to every creature." (Mark 16:15)

What's the most dangerous job in police work? Not the most dangerous assignment, as in Patrol, Vice, Traffic, or SWAT. Any assignment can be dangerous.

Arguably, the most dangerous job in police work is confronting a subject. Whatever your assignment, you're most likely to be wounded or killed when you actually confront a subject. As long as violent criminals are willing to prey on innocent citizens, police work will always be dangerous, and the most dangerous part of the job will always be facing off against the bad guy.

Yet someone has to do it. The mice may all agree that a bell should be put on the cat, but someone has to do the dirty work. On a much larger scale, that's why we have military service. We love our freedoms in America, but someone has to do the dirty work and confront the bad guys who'd love to take those freedoms away.

On a raid or "shots fired" call, you have some prior danger indicators, but on a traffic stop, for instance, you may not. When you approach a subject, you don't know his intentions. He may go easy. He may not. He may be acting smooth, looking for an opening to attack. He may be young, strong, and a better fighter than you. He may not have a gun--until he grabs yours.

Many people seem to forget—or not to care—that when you confront subjects, you're not doing it for fun. You're doing it on behalf of innocent citizens. Without you, most of them would be at the mercy of violent criminals, which is what violent criminals want. So, you have to confront subjects and take the risk.

Yet proactive police work is rewarding because you're doing something important that's bigger than you: helping decent people against predators.

Now look at our opening verse. The Lord Jesus gave this command, the Great Commission, to believers: *"Go ye into all the world, and preach the gospel to every creature."* In other words, tell people wherever you go about Jesus and how to receive Him as Saviour.

Telling people about Jesus is the most important job of a Christian. People are not going to be forgiven for their sins and saved unless someone tells them about Jesus: *"How then shall they call on him* [Jesus] *in whom they have not believed? and how shall they believe in him of whom they have not heard? and how shall they hear without a preacher?"* (Romans 10:14)

In a way, it can be scary; not dangerous scary, but uncertain scary. When you talk with someone about how he needs Jesus, you don't know how he'll react. But it's like confronting criminals. You have to do it.

You may talk with someone who doesn't want to hear about Jesus. Don't think you've wasted your time. *Isaiah 55:11* says, *"So shall my word be that goeth forth out of my mouth: it shall not return unto me void, but it shall accomplish that which I please, and it shall prosper in the thing whereto I sent it."* God's Word will accomplish His work in the heart of the hearer, whether now or later.

Even if someone is not receptive at first, you've planted a seed in his heart by telling him about Jesus: *"I have planted, Apollos watered;"* *(1 Corinthians 3:6)* He may not realize it, but God uses the seed you planted to trouble his conscience about his need for Christ.

You may also speak with someone who has heard the gospel before and he's now more receptive. It's wonderful to share the gospel of Jesus and have someone receive Him as Saviour. His name is now *"...written in heaven." (Luke 10:20)* Also, *"...there is joy in the presence of the angels of God over one sinner that repenteth." (Luke 15:10)* And you rejoice that God let you have a part in it.

When you go to a Bible-believing, soul-winning church and you're active in sharing the gospel, you're also part of something much bigger than you, but it's far more important than arresting criminals. You're *"...labourers together with God:" (1 Corinthians 3:9),* reaching precious souls with the gospel.

God Knows What He's Doing

"Though he slay me, yet will I trust in him:"
(Job 13:15)

As a cop, you see awful things on the job. Ever want to ask God why? Why does a drunk kill or maim an innocent motorist and walk away unhurt? Why do rival gang members shoot at each other and none of them is hurt, but an innocent kid nearby is shot and killed? Why does God let things like that happen?

If anyone had the right to ask God "why", Job did. God allowed some horrible disasters in Job's life. His animals were stolen and destroyed, his servants murdered, his seven sons died in a house collapse, and he was covered with boils. Even his wife told him to give up, *"...curse God, and die." (Job 2:9)* Yet Job said this about God in the midst of his trials: *"Though he slay me, yet will I trust in him:"*

How in the world could Job feel that way?? How could he not shake his fist at God and curse Him? Actually, Job Chapter 1 tells us that's what Satan wanted Job to do. He watched how Job served the Lord and asked God for permission to torment him. God let Satan do his dirty work. Yet God wasn't sitting up in heaven with His fingers crossed. He gave Job the grace he needed to get through this trial.

We can't begin to think on God's level: *"For as the*

heavens are higher than the earth, so are my ways higher than your ways, and my thoughts than your thoughts." (Isaiah 55:9) Yet the Bible doesn't say anywhere that we can't ask God, "Why?"

When God sent Moses to Pharaoh to get the Israelites released, Pharaoh refused and made things worse. Moses asked God, *"Lord, wherefore* ["wherefore" means "why"] *hast thou so evil entreated this people? why is it that thou hast sent me?" (Exodus 5:22)*

When Jeremiah warned of God's judgment upon Judah for sin, he saw people who still enjoyed their sin and he asked God, *"...Wherefore doth the way of the wicked prosper? wherefore are all they happy that deal very treacherously?" (Jeremiah 12:1b)*

If you want to ask God why, the Bible tells us to do two things. One, seek answers in His Word: *"Seek ye out of the book of the LORD, and read:" (Isaiah 34:16)* God speaks to people's hearts through *"...the voice of his word." (Psalm 103:20)*

Two, recognize that God is righteous but tell Him what's on your mind. Before Jeremiah asked God why wicked people prospered, he said, *"Righteous art thou, O LORD, when I plead with thee: yet let me talk with thee of thy judgments:" (Jeremiah 12:1a)*

Job may not have learned why God let him go through those trials, but because there was a Job, there is a book of Job in the Bible. Only God knows how many people throughout history have been helped by this book. It tells us that in tough times, the devil may tempt us to sin, to stop trusting God. Yet God gave Job grace to endure his trials, and He'll do the same for us.

As a cop, you've probably had tough times, and you'll probably have more. Yet you have God's Word that He'll help you just as He helped Job.

We may not see in this life why God lets us go through tough times, but we can trust in him, as Job did. We can be sure that God is righteous, *"The LORD is righteous in all his ways, and holy in all his works." (Psalm 145:17)*

We can also be sure He loves us: *"For God so loved the world, that he gave his only begotten Son, that whosoever believeth on him should not perish, but have everlasting life." (John 3:16)* The best proof of God's love for you is the fact that God the Son, Jesus Christ, died for your sins on the cross, was buried, and rose again.

The Haves and Have Nots

"And he [Jesus] *said unto them, Take heed what ye hear: with what measure ye mete, it shall be measured to you: and unto you that hear shall more be given. For he that hath, to him shall be given: and he that hath not, from him shall be taken even that which he hath."*
(Mark 4:24-25)

Jesus said some people who have something will get more of it, and others who have not will have the little bit that they do have taken away. That doesn't sound fair, does it? Actually, it is fair, and it makes all the sense in the world, when you know what He's talking about.

You may have heard sayings like, "the haves and the have nots" or "the rich get richer and the poor get poorer." Those sayings about riches didn't come from this passage. They may sound similar, but the Lord is not talking about money. He's talking about the knowledge of God.

Just before this passage, the Lord gave the parable of the sower and the seed. The seed represents the Word of God which is sown like seed in people's hearts. Four different kinds of soil are mentioned: the wayside, the shallow ground, the thorny ground, and the good ground. They all represent how people respond to God's Word.

The first soil represents people who hear it but don't want to listen and *"...then cometh the devil, and taketh away the word out of their hearts, lest they should believe and be saved." (Luke 8:12)* They hear how to receive Jesus as Saviour but aren't interested in hearing, so the word is taken away.

The shallow ground represents people who hear the Word and it interests them for a while but their interest doesn't last, especially *"...when tribulation or persecution ariseth because of the word," (Matthew 13:21)* The thorny soil represents others who hear the Word, but their hearts are *"...choked with cares and riches and pleasures of this life," (Luke 8:14)*

Finally, the good ground represents people who, *"...in an honest and good heart, having heard the word, keep it, and bring forth fruit with patience." (Luke 8:15)*

The people on the "good ground" hear that they've sinned against a holy God. They're convicted and uncomfortable, but they listen. They hear how Jesus died for their sins and rose again, and that by coming to Him in repentance and receiving Him by faith as their personal Saviour, they will have forgiveness of sins and eternal life. They make the decision to receive Christ.

Once they are saved, they learn to spend time in God's Word and listen to God's voice as He speaks to their hearts through it. They enjoy it and want more of it and learn more about God: *"...unto you that hear shall more be given."* (Mark 4:24)

People choose in their hearts what kind of "soil" they'll be, whether or not they'll receive God's Word. God said this to the prophet Ezekiel about Israel, who had rebelled terribly against Him,

"Son of man, thou dwellest in the midst of a rebellious house, which have eyes to see, and see not; they have ears to hear, and hear not: for they are a rebellious house." (Ezekiel 12:2)

The problem was not their eyes or their ears, but their heart. They'd decided in their heart that they wouldn't take heed to God's Word.

People choose either to be the spiritual "haves" or "have nots", and "the spiritual rich who get richer" or "the spiritual poor who get poorer." God wants people to enjoy the riches of His salvation and the treasures of His Word, but we have to choose. *"...whosoever will, let him take the water of life freely."* (Revelation 22:17)

The best decision you'll ever make is to receive Jesus as your personal Saviour. The only regret you'll have will be that you hadn't done it sooner.

Hearing Voices

"The Lord GOD hath given me the tongue of the learned, that I should know how to speak a word in season to him that is weary:" (Isaiah 50:4)

Ever get a call like this? *"ANY CAR ABLE TO RESPOND, WE HAVE A CALL OF A MENTAL MALE HEARING VOICES."* That's a scary call. You don't know what you'll find on a call like that. Your guy may just be sad and wants someone to talk to, or he may be soaked in blood with a knife in his hand and a dead body (or more than one) in a house that the voices in his head told him to kill because they were evil.

When you deal with someone who's mentally ill, be kind but cautious. He may not be dangerous for the same reasons a criminal is dangerous, but he can still be dangerous. You may be able to talk him into the car, but if the voices in his head are telling him to fight, you'd better be ready to fight.

You should always handcuff a mental patient when you take him to the hospital. He may be ok one moment, but catapult into a mental health crisis without warning the next. Remember, he's MENTALLY ILL.

If you're a boss on scene (and if you're a boss, you SHOULD be on scene), be the bad guy. Order your officers to cuff him, so they can tell him on the way to the hospital what a jerk you are for making them cuff him. If that helps him to be more cooperative with them and he arrives safely and no one gets hurt, it's ok.

1 Corinthians 14:10 says, *"There are, it may be, so many kinds of voices in the world, and none of them is without signification."* We all "hear voices," not just sounds in our ears but messages that speak to our hearts and minds. The dentist may say, "relax and open wide," but the voice of the drill in his hand is saying, "get ready for pain!" If you're in traffic next to someone blasting his music, you can hear the voice of the motorist, saying, "I don't care about anyone else but myself."

Most of the time, we choose what voices we listen to. Some info is useful. Much of it isn't. Next time you turn on the TV or radio or look up social media, don't just take the "voices" in passively. Think about what you're watching and what's being said. Ask yourself, "Is this worth my time and brainpower?"

Just like all the other voices we hear throughout our day, God has a voice: *"...the voice of his word."* *(Psalm 103:20)* God has many things He wants to tell us, which is one reason why the Bible is as big as it is. *Proverbs 15:23* says, *"...a word spoken in due season, how good is it!"* When you open God's Word, He can speak to your heart in a personal way, and *"...speak a word in season to him that is weary:"*

Police work is a job God ordained: *"...the powers*

that be are ordained of God." "For rulers are not a terror to good works, but to the evil." (Romans 13:1, 3) Yet it's easy to become discouraged and weary with the seemingly endless workload, toxic media, uncaring administration, hostile politics, and other reasons too numerous to mention here. Still, God knows all of them and can help you cope with them.

Ever want to quit? The speaker in *Psalm 94:18-19* apparently did: *"When I said, My foot slippeth;* [he was ready to quit] *thy mercy, O LORD, held me up.* [God *sustained* him]*"* Then he said, *"In the multitude of my thoughts within me* [obviously they were troubled thoughts] *thy comforts delight my soul."*

Amid all the other voices you hear during the day, take time to listen to God's voice. Let Him speak to you and comfort and refresh you. Open His Word and pray, like the psalmist, *"Open thou mine eyes, that I may behold wondrous things out of thy law." (Psalm 119:18)*

Been Around the Block

"He is despised and rejected of men; a man of sorrows, and acquainted with grief: and we hid as it were our faces from him; he was despised, and we esteemed him not. Surely he hath borne our griefs, and carried our sorrows: yet we did esteem him stricken, smitten of God, and afflicted. But he was wounded for our transgressions, he was bruised for our iniquities: the chastisement of our peace was upon him; and with his stripes we are healed. All we like sheep have gone astray; we have turned every one to his own way; and the LORD hath laid on him the iniquity of us all." (Isaiah 53:3-6)

When you hear the name "Jesus Christ", what comes to mind? A man with a soft face, long hair and a beard, a light around his head, and a white robe and red sash like some "hippie picture," as one preacher used to call them? We don't know what Jesus looked like, but He probably didn't look like that.

He probably didn't have long hair. *1 Corinthians 11:14* says, *"Doth not even nature itself teach you, that, if a man have long hair, it is a shame unto him?"* He'd been a carpenter- *"Is not this the carpenter,"* (Mark 6:3)—so He probably looked rugged from hard work. He did have a beard. It was ripped out after His arrest: *"I gave my back to the smiters, and my cheeks to them that plucked off the hair:"* (Isaiah 50:6)

303

What Jesus looked like doesn't really matter, though. What matters is what Jesus did. *John 21:25* says, *"And there are also many other things which Jesus did, the which, if they should be written every one, I suppose that even the world itself could not contain the books that should be written. Amen."*

So the world can't contain all the info about Jesus, but here's one thing that will help you immensely as a cop: the fact that Jesus was *"...a man of sorrows, and acquainted with grief:"* Before His birth, Jesus existed as God and was worshipped by angels: *"And let all the angels of God worship him." (Hebrews 1:6)* But He came to earth and was *"...despised and rejected of men;"* People despised and rejected Him.

Our passage says Jesus *"...hath borne our griefs, and carried our sorrows:"* Whatever makes us sad, Jesus has gone through it. The Bible doesn't tell everything Jesus did. If it did, the Bible would be a lot thicker than it is.

It tells some things, like how He healed people and raised the dead and *"...went about doing good," (Acts 10:38)* and how the religious leaders kept trying to trip Him up and destroy Him and some tried to kill Him, in spite of all the good He did.

Jesus wasn't some effeminate sissy. He was a real man who knew plenty about trouble and sorrow. He *"...hath borne our griefs, and carried our sorrows:"*

Ultimately, He endured a brutal death to pay for our sins: *"But he was wounded for our transgressions, he was bruised for our iniquities: the chastisement of our peace was upon him; and with his stripes we are healed."*

Yet Jesus didn't stay dead. He rose again: *"I am he that liveth, and was dead; and, behold, I am alive for evermore, Amen;"* *(Revelation 1:18)* Later *"...he was received up into heaven, and sat on the right hand of God." (Mark 16:19)* So even though we can't see, hear, or touch Him, Jesus is alive.

How does that help you on the job? Well, cops deal with grievous things that most people never see. When something happens you have trouble dealing with, it helps to talk with someone who gets it, who's been through it, and can strengthen and help you with his counsel. Jesus is Someone you can go to. He's alive. He gets it. He can help. You go to Him by prayer. He gives you counsel with His Word, the Bible.

You may go through grievous times most people don't understand, but there's nothing in the world that Jesus doesn't understand and can't help you with.

Learning to Forgive

"And when they were come to the place, which is called Calvary, there they crucified him, and the malefactors, one on the right hand, and the other on the left. Then said Jesus, Father, forgive them; for they know not what they do. And they parted his raiment, and cast lots." (Luke 23:33-34)

Jesus has been convicted in a sham trial and taken to the governor Pontius Pilate to be put to death. Pilate knew Jesus was innocent: *"For he knew that for envy they had delivered him." (Matthew 27:18)* Yet the religious leaders got the crowd to demand His death: *"But the chief priests and elders persuaded the multitude that they should ask Barabbas, and destroy Jesus." (Matthew 27:20)*

In the end, Pilate did the politically convenient thing: he gave them what they wanted to save his own career.

Jesus is now on the cross--a bloody, gory mass of flesh: *"...his visage was so marred more than any man, and his form more than the sons of men:" (Isaiah 52:14)* His bones are visible: *"...they pierced my hands and my feet. I may tell all my bones:" (Psalm 22:16-17)* He's dehydrated: *"My strength is dried up like a potsherd; and my tongue cleaveth to my jaws;" (Psalm 22:15)* They mock His suffering: *"He saved others; himself he cannot save." (Matthew 27:42)* The soldiers gamble for His clothing: *"...They parted my raiment*

among them, and for my vesture they did cast lots."
(John 19:25)

He could have stopped all this! He'd told His captors at His arrest, *"Thinkest thou that I cannot now pray to my Father, and he shall presently give me more than twelve legions of angels?" (Matthew 26:53)*

Yet even on the cross, He never asked punishment on those who'd plotted His death, or the soldiers or guards or the crowd. He asked forgiveness for them all, even hanging in agony as people mocked Him.

People challenged Him to come down from the cross. Talk about literally playing with fire! Yet if He'd come down, then no one—us included—could be forgiven for sins and escape hell.

Jesus knew how bad hell is. He'd created it *"...for the devil and his angels:" (Matthew 25:41)* He died for our sins so we could be forgiven and saved and not go to hell. When He died, our sin-debt was paid in full. That's why He said, *"It is finished:" (John 19:30)* before He died. The third day, He rose from the grave victoriously!

If you know Jesus as Saviour, you already know all this. Yet take time now and then to think of what Jesus did for you; how all your sins were put on Him: *"...the LORD hath laid on him the iniquity of us all." (Isaiah 53:6)* Even when you're saved, it's easy to forget Jesus' love and sacrifice. Take time to think now and then about who saved you and what He saved you from:

"Hearken to me, ye that follow after righteousness, ye that seek the LORD: look unto the rock whence ye are hewn, and to the hole of the pit whence ye are digged." (Isaiah 51:1)

"Lest I forget Gethsemane, lest I forget thine agony, Lest I forget thy love for me, lead me to Calvary."
"Lead me to Calvary"
Jennie Evelyn Hussey, William J. Kirkpatrick

Focusing on Jesus will help you to be more grateful to Him for saving you and more enthusiastic about serving Him. It will also help you forgive others who do you wrong: *"And be ye kind one to another, tenderhearted, forgiving one another, even as God for Christ's sake hath forgiven you." (Ephesians 4:32)*

As a cop, you'll probably be burned at some point, and probably more than once: perhaps by bosses, the media, politicians, or other cops. God can give you grace to forgive others' wrongs, as Jesus has forgiven you all your wrongdoings since you received Him.

You may not know Jesus as Saviour. You may think your sins are too bad for God to forgive you. Yet look at how Jesus was toward His tormentors! If He was willing to forgive them, He's certainly willing to forgive you!

Things have Changed; God Hasn't

"Who is left among you that saw this house in her first glory? and how do ye see it now? is it not in your eyes in comparison of it as nothing? Yet now be strong, O Zerubbabel, saith the LORD; and be strong, O Joshua, son of Josedech, the high priest; and be strong, all ye people of the land, saith the LORD, and work: for I am with you, saith the LORD of hosts:"
(Haggai 2:3-4)

A little background on this passage: God had let the Babylonians take Judah into captivity for their continual sin against God. The Babylonians destroyed Jerusalem and the temple. This captivity lasted seventy years. Eventually the Babylonians were defeated by the Medes and Persians. Cyrus the Persian king let the Jews return to their homeland and rebuild the temple.

At the time of this writing, the Jews have just laid the foundation of the new temple. Looking at our passage, Zerubbabel was the governor of Judah. Joshua (not the Joshua who led Israel after Moses) was the high priest.

When the foundation of the post-captivity temple was laid, many older Jews were there who'd seen the previous temple that King Solomon had built. According to *Ezra 3:12, "...when the foundation of this house* [the post-captivity temple] *was laid before their eyes,"* many of the older Jews *"... wept with a loud voice;"*

Why did they cry? Verse 3 of our passage gives a clue: *"Who is left among you that saw this house in her first glory? and how do ye see it now? is it not in your eyes in comparison of it as nothing?"* Maybe they were sad that the new temple would not be nearly so splendid as the old.

Yet God assured them that no matter the size of the temple, they still had Him: *"...be strong, all ye people of the land, saith the LORD, and work: for I am with you, saith the LORD of hosts:"* It was a new time, but God was still God.

Here's the application: if you have, say, twenty years or more as a cop, you may be like the older Jews, in a way. You remember how the job was "when you were allowed to do police work", and how it is now with all the restrictions, micromanagement, and toxic media.

You may be discouraged that cops can't do what they could before, and how criminals take advantage, and decent people in bad areas suffer: a fact which many people in power who set policy just can't seem to get.

What do you do, then? Quit? Let criminals run the streets? Don't you dare. Restrictions or not, you may be the only defense these citizens have, and you know it and they know it. So do your best work and encourage younger officers to do their best.

Things aren't like they were, but God is still on His

throne. Police work is still a job He ordained, no matter what anyone says to the contrary. If people in power set bad policy or generate a toxic environment for cops and for decent people, that's their sin, not yours.

Likewise, if you're a Christian, don't just lament about how bad things are nowadays. Jesus Christ still forgives sins, saves souls, and changes lives. The Bible is still true. God still answers prayer. The Great Commission is still in effect. God meant it when He said, *"...I am with you, saith the LORD of hosts:"*

Just like He was with the post-captivity people, He's with us, too. So, trust His Word, share His gospel, and *"...be strong, all ye people of the land, saith the LORD, and work: for I am with you, saith the LORD of hosts:"*

Made in USA - North Chelmsford, MA

01.19.2021 0132